Happy

by Amanda Talbot

Photography by Josef S. Rosemann

MURDOCH BOOKS

Contents

Contents

HAPPINESS
IS THE MEANING
AND
THE PURPOSE OF LIFE,
THE WHOLE AIM AND
THE END OF HUMAN
EXISTENCE.

Aristotle, *Ethics*

About happiness

The only thing most of us want is to be happy. I came to this conclusion in 2012, when I wrote my previous book, *Rethink: The Way You Live*. After researching major living trends around the world I realised that, although there were different tribes of people taking various paths, they all had one goal – they wanted to be happy. It was an 'aha' moment for me. For many years I have investigated how good and bad design can affect our emotions, so it suddenly became obvious that if all we really want in life is happiness, then surely design can play a vital role.

Over the years I've visited institutions for the sick and the homeless and I have seen how buildings that are poorly designed can agitate and frustrate people and even prolong illness. So, what happens if we create spaces that are calming and soothing, which provoke confidence, empathy, security, pride, creativity or motivation? Surely this could help us on the path to happiness?

When I began researching this book, the first thing I decided to do was to hold my own 'Happy Poll'. I wanted to understand what people

About happiness

around the world thought about happiness, and if they thought good design could make them happy. I surveyed 166 people from all walks of life, from several countries, so I could be armed with my own data to help me better understand people's needs. I put together 132 questions about home life and sent it out through social media and via an email campaign. All sorts of people responded, including university students, twenty-somethings, single parents, stay-at-home parents, working parents, high achievers in business and people who were unemployed. Before completing the Happy Poll, prospective participants were asked to complete the Oxford Happiness Questionnaire – developed by scientists at Oxford University – to help assess their current state of happiness. My dream is to collate all of this information and one day create the ultimate Happy Home. I am already calling it the Happy Home Project.

In the Happy Poll, when I asked people, 'What is happiness to you?', there was a variety of answers that came up again and again: feeling content, love, not being stressed, not being restricted by finances when making life choices, being debt-free, living a balanced lifestyle, spending time with loved ones, family and friends, laughter, enjoying good health, having a meaningful life, feeling fulfilled, peace, having free time, sunshine, a glass of wine and even just coffee.

Defining happiness is like trying to define what is beautiful and what is ugly. The topic is subjective and multilayered. What may appear unattractive to the eye can still bring overwhelming happiness. For example, I bought my husband a golden rabbit ornament to celebrate Easter in the first apartment we shared together in London. Every time my friends come to visit they always remark how ugly it is. The thing is, it gives my husband and me great pleasure and, yes, it does make us happy every time we see it!

As British design and life commentator Stephen Bayley says, what is one person's happiness can be another person's misery. He once told me in an interview, 'cheerful music makes me suicidal. I can't stand cheerful tunes but I guess some find enjoyment in them'.

The pursuit of happiness

Happy interiors are about way more than just being decorated in bright colours.

Through my research I have found there are a lot of people who are uneasy with the word 'happiness' – and I'm not talking about pessimists or people who have lived in great hardship. When discussing the concept for my book, people were so uncomfortable they would wriggle in their chair and became visibly unhappy. At one dinner party, the debate was so heated that one diner blurted out, 'There is no such thing as happiness and the idea of pursuing it will only make us miserable!'

My dining companion could be partly right, because much research suggests that the act of seeking out happiness can actually make us unhappy. 'It is the very pursuit of happiness that thwarts happiness,' said Viktor Frankl, twentieth-century Viennese psychiatrist and neurologist. But maybe this is because our approach has been wrong and we are looking for happiness in the wrong places.

Happy

A big problem in our modern western world is that we tend to measure our happiness by the work we do and the material success it brings. However, no matter how wealthy we are, the 'pursuit of happiness' impulse is always there, urging us to find bigger, better and shinier things, wishing we lived in that house or drove that car. It's rare that we make happiness about simply savouring the moment, making the most of what we have, or putting energy and love into the space we live in.

Are we fruitlessly striving for the promised land of lasting happiness? One of the world's leading researchers into the subject of 'happiness', Dan Gilbert of Harvard University, has found we are terrible at predicting what will lead to happiness. You would assume that winning the lottery would make our happiness levels skyrocket, while a spinal cord injury would make them plummet. But this is not always the case.

Since 1972, only about a third of Americans have described themselves as 'very happy'. And, since 2004, the number of Americans who identify themselves as optimists has plummeted from 79 to 50 per cent. In the Happy Poll, 12 per cent of people said they felt they were pessimists and 33 per cent said they are not as happy as they expected to be at this stage of their life.

Industrial designer Marc Sadler cycling in front of his Milan studio.

Fifty per cent of our happiness is genetic and unchangeable, says Professor Sonja Lyubomirsky of the University of California, following an extensive study on twins. Only 10 per cent of happiness depends on life circumstances such as levels of income and health. The remaining 40 per cent is what we can change. This 40 per cent is what I want to explore and discuss in this book. I want to demonstrate the effects of using good design in our homes and communities, and show how it can help us live a happier life.

Is there such a thing as 'happy design'?

Have you ever searched online for images of 'happy interiors'? The results aren't pretty, and very few of those examples make me feel happy. The main flaw with many people's idea of happy design is they oversimplify the meaning. When they think of a happy design, they visualise something bright, bold, childlike and maybe a little tacky. There's a lot of bad-taste design out there that provides an endless supply of gimmicky shopping-mall-like buildings and nasty residential developments. Like sugar, they give you a temporary boost, but ultimately they're debilitating. Certain fast-food chains come to mind. Historically, these restaurants were designed to make us feel upbeat, but the decor was also designed to get you out of there as quickly as possible! This is how I used to feel about what I also thought were 'happy' interiors. I would try to avoid them because they made me uncomfortable. I couldn't relax in them and they seemed to be yelling at me. Interestingly, Stephen Bayley told me that legendary designer Sir Terence Conran famously described design items he didn't care for as 'unhappy'.

After spending a year reading the science and psychology behind happiness and travelling across the globe to visit some remarkable homes,

What makes you happy?

A simple technique that helps you focus on what makes a happy home for you is to write a list of all the activities you love doing. This can be anything from watching the sunset to having a long bath. For example, if you like the piano, then why not have a grand piano in the centre of a large living room, especially as new technology makes it possible to soundproof the room? If you like books, then why not have a house in which all the walls are bookshelves? If you like cooking, why not have a large kitchen where you can also entertain? Once you have jotted down your list then you need to give yourself one month per item on the list to incorporate these ideas into the design of your home. This simple exercise helps you to be more conscious of what makes you happy, and to prioritise these things in your personal space.

designs and people, I am more confident than ever that happy design is an idea we should explore. And the good news is I have discovered that those preconceptions about happy design are now outdated.

But what about the Happy Home? Who would be bold enough to say they have created one, and how on earth would we recreate it? I mean, surely happiness in our home design is related to our own personal taste and experiences? People in the Happy Poll certainly seemed to think so: 77 per cent believed it was possible to achieve happiness through good design and architecture. On the flipside, a badly designed home tended to make people unhappy, especially things like: lack of storage, lack of space, too much clutter, not enough space for alone time, no garden, noise, lack of light, outdated interiors and furniture.

Historically, the words 'design' and 'happy' have not really been used together. Instead, pragmatism tended to be of paramount importance to design, and was how designers justified themselves and their values. Design and architectural courses teach the importance of wellbeing, so why has it been so hard for many people, even in the design world, to believe that a home or product can make you feel happy?

You achieve feel-good design when you create spaces and objects people enjoy using.

Although our sense of wellbeing – or happiness, in other words – has always been an extremely important subtext, it is now celebrated as an essential component in its own right within design. Architects and designers are starting to use terms like 'soulful', 'emotional', 'creative', 'beautiful', 'heartfelt' and 'joyful' to describe their designs. Some designers still don't want to use the word 'happy', but are also creating spaces and objects that they want us to enjoy, so I'm more than comfortable to call these happy designs too.

Happy design is not just about function and form, it's about making you feel good.

We are seeing a growing number of designers approaching happy design in different ways. Designers are looking at aesthetic or tactile interpretations of happiness. They are using incredible colours, textures, quality of materials and finishes. Their joyous work plays to our emotions, and speaks to our hearts as much as to our heads. Understanding the complexities of what makes humans happy, and the possibilities for using this knowledge to build cities, homes and objects that can enhance our daily wellbeing, is a very exciting prospect.

Accept the challenge and get happy

I believe – as does a growing group of scientists, architects, designers and other creative people – that thoughtful design can contribute to growing confidence, boosting optimism, reducing stress, improving relationships and helping to conquer negative thoughts. In *Happy,* I want to show you the possibilities for your life: at home, in the community and in our built environment.

However, before we charge after something, we first need to think long and hard about whether it will make us happy. I detest fashion for its lightning-speed changes and the powerful influence it can have over us. Every day we are fed new evocative images of must-have products. Life has got so noisy with information telling us how we should be living,

About happiness

Focus on all the little details to create those smile-on-your-face moments.

that there's rarely time to take stock and ask, 'What makes me tick?', 'What makes me feel good?', or even 'Who am I?'

While working on the book, I lost one of the most important people in my life: my grandfather. He was my rock. He was the most brilliant, yet uncomplicated, person I know. He inspired my love of nature, the ocean and handmade objects as well as my obsession in seeing how houses can be turned from sad to happy spaces – my grandparents were nomads who constantly moved into rundown houses and transformed them into family homes. Most of my happy childhood memories are of being with him. I would spend hours every day in his garage watching him make beautiful objects from humble timber. He always helped me make whatever I imagined, including an upright surfboard bookshelf! For one of my birthdays, he even surprised me with my own cubby house. I'm not talking about any old house; it was the envy of everyone who visited us.

I was away in Europe on the photoshoot for this book when my mum called me from Australia to tell me the devastating news of my grandad's death. He died exactly one year after the passing of my nana – one of the most amazing women I have ever met. I can't explain the pain, but I know those of you who have lost someone will understand.

Shortly after receiving the sad news, the photographer and I arrived at one of the most beautiful homes I have ever been to, owned by a generous and warm Swiss couple, Mirko Beetschen and Stéphane Houlmann. The way the space was designed relaxed me. It exposed me. I had tried to stay strong despite what had happened, but I just crumbled. Sitting on a window ledge looking out, with a fire blazing in the fireplace and a blanket wrapped around me, I welled up. In a place that made me feel at home, all I wanted to do was be home – the place where my memories and loved ones were.

I never imagined that working on *Happy* was going to be one of the saddest times in my life. But I believe the pain and anguish I felt made me focus on the need for this book, and how it could really make a difference to people's lives.

I decided to take the Oxford Happiness Questionnaire. My Happy Index score was 3.2. The average score is 4 plus, so the results were telling. Admittedly this was a sad time for me, but when I told people my score they were shocked, because I usually have a big fat smile across my face. It also seemed crazy to me as I have so much to be grateful for. I realised I was the perfect person on whom to test my theories in this book. I will be honest; some of the changes I made were much harder than I could have possibly imagined. I had moments when I wept uncontrollably while writing *Happy*. I know this seems weird, as who has a breakdown writing about happiness? But it made me analyse myself and the burdens I have put on myself, and led me to understand the need to accept who I am.

But the thing is, I have experienced a change. Real change. My Happy Index score is now above 5. This has been the most incredible journey I have ever been on. What I thought I knew about happy design wasn't even close to the mark. I knew the theories, but it was another thing to actually put them into practice.

Happy

I want to challenge you to step away from what, or who, is influencing you – such as magazines or social media – for one month or longer, and refocus on you. Listen to yourself. Find your own identity. Just like someone who cuts off all their hair as a symbol of a fresh start, cut yourself off and rediscover what in your home has true meaning to you. Yes, it might take time and effort, and I know it's often easier to be told what to do, but the truth is you will never find lasting contentment if you choose other people's inspirations.

It is up to you to design your home to support a way of life that appeals to you. I believe the perfectly designed building displays optimism, self-confidence, gratitude, hope, compassion, purpose and empathy – these are all qualities any design can have. You just have to learn how. And doing so will change your life.

But remember – and I hate to tell you this – you are not perfect and, no matter how hard you try, there are going to be days when you feel sad. The idea of finding eternal happiness isn't realistic. I mean, we are mortals, after all. If there wasn't sadness in the world, how could there be happiness? How could we design spaces or products if we never experience tragedy, heartache or hard times? It's often the very dark times that have helped me appreciate the true meaning of happiness.

When we are designing spaces to live in, we need to create corners, areas, nooks or rooms that can accommodate all our moods. If we design a space that is 'up', 'buzzy' and 'energetic' all the time, it doesn't give us room to breathe or experience the way we are feeling. Negative emotions are an important ingredient for having meaningful experiences and achieving happiness. It's up to you to create a space to comfort you in those times.

Some people have argued with me that it's not possible to achieve happiness through design. However, I believe that the ideas in this book will make you happier. I want the house you are living in, or are about to renovate, decorate or move into, to be the happiest place you have ever lived in. The beautiful photographs of the amazing places I have visited are included to inspire you and help illustrate the ideas.

I'm definitely not saying that the ideas, people, homes and designs in this book are The Answer to finding happiness. All these people, just like you and I, have bad days, are not always content and are in no way 'happiness crusaders'. They have been chosen for their honesty and their brilliant vision for design and architecture.

The ideas in this book will not make you thinner, richer or help you find the perfect partner. What they will do is help get your home right. And I'm a firm believer that once you get your home right, the other stuff will probably get sorted out too. Your home should make you feel recharged and rejuvenated, and restore you to the highest version of the person you are meant to be. It should make you feel happy.

I don't want *Happy* to be a wishy-washy self-help book, but understanding the need to be authentic in who we are can change the way we live and, ultimately, design our lives, homes and communities. This is a ride. Stick with it, because I know it could change your life.

The happiness curve

Lifetime happiness trends are shaped a little like a smile. People are happiest in their youth and golden years. Joy dips in middle age, but people become more content again after around 50.

I

Colour

COLOUR IS LIFE. LIVING WITHOUT COLOUR IS LIKE REFUSING TO LIVE.

Matali Crasset, designer

Colour your world

Amanda on
the power of colour,
colour trends
& defining happy colours

When we think of happiness, we can often relate it to colour. Can you imagine a world with no colour? A forest, ocean or sky only in black and white would be dull and depressing. Whenever we open our eyes we are surrounded by colour. We see it in nature, from the changing hues of the sky to the myriad tones of the plant kingdom and the animal world, and in our human-made environments, too – in public buildings, houses, streets and cars. It's everywhere.

Artist Katharina Grosse's Berlin atelier has a cheery patchwork curtain that softens the Brutalist staircase designed by Augustin und Frank Architekten.

Colour

Colour has as strong an impact as smell and sound. French architect Le Corbusier claimed that colour 'is an element as necessary as water and fire'. It is vital to our visual perception and how we experience our environment. It can even communicate ideas to us. Certain colours such as red suggest warning, while we have come to associate the colour green with safety – think traffic lights. It's also been found that most people often make a judgement about a product, or even a place or person, based on colour alone.

Colour is the power tool when it comes to design. It can make or break a space. It can change your mood, making you feel happy, sad, energetic or relaxed. It can even bring people together, with vibrant warm tones being the ideal backdrop for a place to gather and have fun, while cooling, calming hues are great for a space for the family to chill out and relax in. Having saturated hues around us every day can provide inspiration, make us think faster, make us feel hungry or, of course, happy.

Augustin und Frank have made artist Katharina Grosse's kitchen in her Berlin home a warming focal point of the minimalist interior, by introducing a fun palette to the units.

I can't help but feel we haven't fully embraced fun colours in our interiors since the 1970s, a decade famous for social freedom and the pursuit of a good time. Over the past few years we have been taking our interiors way too seriously, so much so that we can't see past neutrals, grey, white and black. We need to stop avoiding using bright colours in our homes. I'm not suggesting we should turn our homes into a seventies tribute – there were certainly some 'OMG, this isn't good' moments in home decor back then. Thankfully, our appreciation of

aesthetics and quality continues to develop as more people become aware of design. What we could embrace from that era, though, is the freedom and fun.

Designer Mark Tuckey proves colour can be beautiful when used on natural materials such as timber.

When it comes to understanding colour, I am a big believer in not following fads, but learning to approach the subject in an holistic, human-centric way. For too long, colour in architecture and interior design was simply thought of as decorative, but it can play a much more powerful role. The colour of a building or space should connect the inside with the outside and, more importantly, connect it with the humans who live there or use it.

Don't limit colour to your walls and accessories. A bold hue on the floor can ground the foundation of an interior.

From the beginning of the design process, you should be aware of the emotions, feelings and moods you want a space to have. Good colour choice in design is an essential factor in the communication between human beings and architectural space in all areas of life.

French designer Matali Crasset is a strong believer in using colour in homes and buildings. Her Paris home is a living colour laboratory.

If you are not confident with colour, create a colour palette of three to five shades and stick with it. As you get braver, you can introduce new hues to the space.

COLOUR
Agenda

Optimistic colour

I find it exciting to see that architects aren't exclusively using colour inside the home to express themselves, but are using it in urban developments to cheer not only those who live there, but the whole neighbourhood.

In cities of uninterrupted grey buildings against a backdrop of continuous grey skies, endless grey footpaths and never-ending dreary grey roads, there isn't a more sunny relief than a building that pops with colour to break the monotony. When cities embrace colour, they are showing their citizens and visitors that this is a place of confidence, self-assurance and buoyancy. In Kolkata in 2012, the government decided that certain public buildings and structures would be painted sky blue. The colour was chosen for both its beauty and ability to soothe. In 2006, a similar decision was taken in Aurangabad in Bihar, one of India's poorest states with a high crime rate. The façades of the buildings were painted pink in a bid to reduce crime and to lift morale.

On the downside, it's risky when large developments are covered in on-trend colours because those trends will disappear, making a once-attractive place to live feel dated. And, if colour is used in neighbourhoods suffering from poverty or crime, those shades subconsciously become identified with the areas, preventing other neighbourhoods from using them.

This is why I love German designer Werner Aisslinger's utopian vision for the 'home of the future'. He took over the Haus am Waldsee museum in Berlin in April 2013 and temporarily covered the façade of the historic building with a multicoloured patchwork fabric. His aim was to explore how interchangeable 'clothing' for a building can modify its look and feel rather than the colour and patterns remaining permanent fixtures.

What are happy colours?

When I began the process of writing *Happy* I believed I could create the perfect Happy Colour Palette. I quickly learnt that it was impossible to pinpoint happy colours, because what is one person's happy colour can be another person's living nightmare. Humans are complex and diverse, so it isn't possible for there to be just one colour solution for everybody. Colour is personal and is also closely tied to memory. In our past we may have forged a connection with certain colours – for instance, because of the colour of a favourite toy from our childhood. We all have our own 'colour fingerprint'. When it comes to colour you need to trust your own instincts. As fashion designer Coco Chanel said, 'The best colour in the whole world is the one that looks good on you'.

Generally, the colours most people consider 'happy' are block primary colours like blue, yellow, red, green and orange. As fun as these colours are, and they certainly do pack a punch, they can sometimes scream for attention, which is not great for the home environment. Primary colours are too bright for most adults and generally lack the sophistication people are wanting for their home.

I think where we go wrong is we forget about the colours that make us feel calm, relaxed, soothed or restful. We have labelled these feelings as 'wellbeing', but I think wellbeing and happiness belong in the same box. If you use colours that make you feel calm or good, then surely they are going to make you feel happy. I don't believe happiness is only the moments of excitement, adrenaline and laughing out loud. Some of my happiest times are when I'm curled up on my sofa, sitting quietly and calmly.

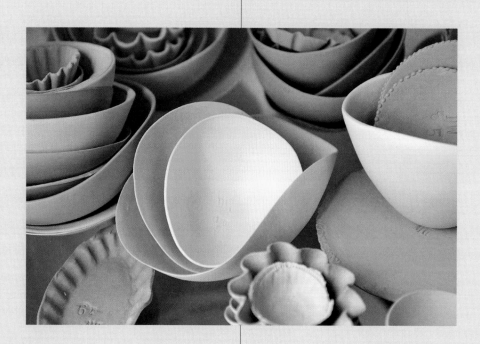

The ultimate happy palette

Dulux Australia kindly helped me by conducting a small survey in June 2013 about colour and emotions. Six palettes of various colours were created. More than 100 people were surveyed, and were shown the six colour palettes. They were asked, 'Which emotion do you most strongly feel when looking at each colour palette?' The possible emotions were: calm, happy, excited, positive or none of these. However, when I saw the palette that Dulux put together following the research, it didn't make me happy. I felt as though the palette represented what people have been conditioned to think happy colours are. It included the obvious choices like yellow, purple, orange and shades of blue.

I then turned my home into a Dulux laboratory and discovered that the colours that made me feel good in my kitchen and living room were Happy yellow, Colony green and Shy Girl pink, balanced with white, silver, grey and gold. But these are my personal choices and I know that for many of you the very thought of living with these would not put a smile on your face.

However, the one colour that most people seem to agree on is the Mr Happy of the colour world – yellow. Yellow makes you think of sunshine and has been found to trigger the release of the feel-good brain chemical serotonin. If you need to add one sure happy colour into your life, it is this cheerful hue. The trick I have found to keep yellow a happy shade – and not one that gives you a migraine – is to contain it. It works amazingly well when used as a colour tool for the unexpected. For example, use it inside your cupboards, so that each time you open a door it's almost like a ray of sunshine is escaping. Or use it as a block colour for a staircase.

Inspiration from nature

When it comes to colour, nature is always my starting point. When using natural hues, I find that – just like smell, sound and touch – they transport me to a moment, a memory. I'm not just talking blue skies and green trees. I'm talking about those *epic* moments that we usually only see for a split second. It's in those moments we can be inspired to create something breathtakingly beautiful.

I'm personally a believer that when using colour in your home you should combine it with natural materials. Often colour fails within interiors because it's too brash and harsh. But when you introduce it to wool, linen, cotton, timber or stone, it can soften the shade and make it more tactile, approachable and harmonious.

After the recent global financial crisis, people lost confidence in just about everything and wanted to go back to basics. Natural timbers and soothing white ceramics and stone were mixed together with raw silver, bronze and copper metals. Now the mood has moved again. A growth in handmade is also taking place, so perfection is a thing of the past. Bold brushstrokes, uneven printing and digital merged with handpainted are making an entrance into our psyche. Due to our growing concern for the environment, shades of green and blue are also here to stay. People are learning how to work with sometimes difficult colours by mixing shades just as Mother Nature does – rather than sticking to one continuous colour, as so many decorating shows tell us we must.

By looking outside, Jean-Christophe Aumas found his inspiration for creating the perfect colour palette for his upbeat Paris apartment.

'I haven't really made mistakes with colour. It's more that I have liked the outcome less than I thought I would. I keep on learning.'
— Ghislaine Viñas, interior designer

Colour confidence

Over the years I have come to realise that using colour gives you confidence, and the confidence you have in yourself and your home tends to result in happiness.

One of the best things about colour is that it's a small investment to make to help you enjoy your home. It's an easy way of making the very most of your interior. But there are so many people who don't play with colour due to fear. Common concerns I hear when talking to people about designing with colour in the home are, 'What if I fail?', 'What if it looks ugly once it's on my walls?' or 'What if I get it horribly wrong?' Believe me, I hear this kind of talk all the time. Stop that way of thinking right now! Instead of expecting failure, expect success! Stop assuming the worst.

You must experiment. You must play with colour. It's about making mistakes and learning. It's about your willingness to try things out and your capacity to learn. If you do go down the wrong path, treat it as an opportunity to practise and know that next time will be better.

Interestingly, our colour confidence seems to change with the seasons. In warm summer months we generally feel more open to colour, and experiment with bolder options such as pinks and fluoro yellows. But in winter months we retreat and hibernate, and we opt for safe greys. Why should colour be abandoned because of the time of year? Winter is just the time to embrace colour in our life – and I'm not talking small highlights or complementary touches. If anything, you should bring more colour into your home in the darker months. Then,

when you are hot and bothered in the warmer months, you could choose more soothing, cooling colours.

When you use colour with confidence it says something about your character. You are showing that you are strong, capable and something that many others long to be. Believing it is the key to living it.

I can tell you that a door painted in a colour other than white, greige or black is inviting, warming and cheerful. Colour queen of New York, Ghislaine Viñas, has created the Sky House with a vivid orange doorway, and it's one of the friendliest doors you could possibly walk through. It wasn't the obvious colour choice but it looks damn cool and inviting, and somehow you just know the people inside have taste and are fun. As adults, so many of us want to give the appearance that we are sophisticated and elegant, and we do seem to opt for safe, conservative choices to achieve this. The thing is, you can still be all of those things when you introduce colour into your life.

There aren't really any no-nos when it comes to decorating with colour. It's an amazing tool to use to hide your architectural mistakes. If you are wary of using new bold tones, the best advice is to make brave colour statements in your home mixed with the classic tones that you feel more confident with.

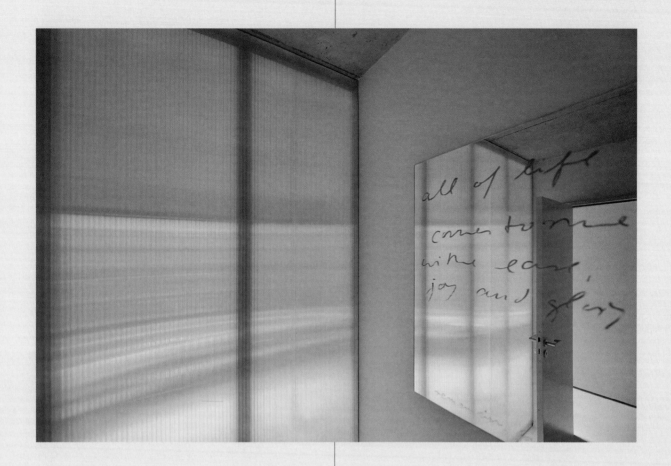

Colour for health

Colour can make a huge difference to your health and happiness. Using colour to heal is not a modern concept. In ancient Greece patients were 'colour-diagnosed' and then placed in a temple radiating the prescribed hue. Today we are starting to see a rise in design professionals using colour to help with healing in healthcare settings.

Colour is very important to mental health. It's true; the world does look grey when you are depressed. Depressed or anxious people are more likely to associate their mood with grey, while happier people tend to prefer yellow. Also, research has shown that when we are depressed, contrasts of colours can appear to be dulled. Therefore, if you are designing a space for someone who suffers from dark moods, look at shades that will brighten up a space.

Research by British retailer Littlewoods has even shown that people with grey bedrooms tend to have sex 1.8 times per week, as opposed to 3.49 per week for those with purple walls!

However, as much as I want you to use colour, it's important to learn to understand it. Where so many people go wrong with pigment is they create environments that are too loud, bold and brash. Intensive colour stimuli covering a large area can lead to severe visual fatigue. It is important to take into consideration the amount of colour stimulus (degree of colourfulness) and stimuli variations (contrasts) that are beneficial to the individual's health and wellbeing.

Colour and emotion

Colours are powerful. Research is proving that they can tap into our emotions and affect us physiologically and psychologically. They have an effect on our emotions, which act on hormones and neurotransmitters, the chemical messengers in our brain, and this in turn changes the way our bodies feel and behave.

In the 1960s, Swiss psychotherapist Max Lüscher theorised that human feelings regarding certain colours are based on human experiences with that hue. His research found that the common association of tranquillity with green may be the result of nomadic peoples' use of green forests as an escape, offering safety from the open fields and sunlight, where they would be visible. The forest was more than likely considered a place of rest and recovery, similar to the way we see our homes today. His work suggests that 'survival has meant understanding what nature is telling us and communicating to us through colour'. Many of the world's best colour experts use Lüscher's studies as a guide for their design selections.

Although colour has such an emotional hold on us I have found people are more inclined to decorate their home in the latest fashion hue rather than deciding on the emotional state they want to feel. This is a pity.

When New York interior designer Ghislaine Viñas uses hints of neon in a room, it's like adding an exclamation mark at the end of a sentence.

Chapter One

Colour is your best weapon for creating surprise, fun, humour and happiness – as well as a cool vibe – in your new happy home.

Remember...

Non-primary colours are more calming than primary colours
• Blue is the most calming of the primaries, followed closely by
light red • Too much of a good thing, including loud colours
like yellow, orange and red, can cause too much negative visual
stimulation • Being understimulated is just as harmful as being
overstimulated, so always add another hue to your neutrals
• One colour can't provoke a mood – you need at least two to
stimulate the senses • When only using neutrals it is imperative
to combine them with patterns and texture

'The absence of colour makes me unhappy. When only careless greys or whites are used, I can't find anything to resonate with in a building.'
— Jean-Christophe Aumas, creative director

Colour and mood
word association

A fun exercise is to select a word for the mood or emotion you want for a space. Explain what you think that word evokes, and then write down the colours that seem to match. For me, when I think of the following moods, this is what I imagine.

ICONIC Iconic colours are deeply rooted in history, maybe related to a country or a historical moment that changed the way we live. These colours tend to be strong and rich and should be used boldly. They should be impressive and even overwhelming and can work on a large scale. I think of royal blue connected to the royal family, Tiffany & Co.'s minty blue or charcoal grey for Brutalist architecture.

GENEROUS When it comes to generosity, it's impossible for me not to relate this word to food. Generosity is all about deep, warmer, darker tones. I think of root vegetables and autumnal tones: plum, forest green, dark orange, mustards and rusty reds.

EMPATHIC When I think of this word, it's about openness, understanding and being warm-hearted, while being calm and collected at the same time. I imagine cooler, lighter blues, greens, white, soft greys and charcoal.

PLAYFUL I associate this with the outdoors, being at the beach or park, bathed in sunshine. The mood is warm, friendly and full of smiles. A playful palette is not necessarily bold and loud – think sensual, lively hues or cool icy blues, silver, gold, sunshine yellow or sky blue breaking out into a spritely neutral backdrop.

LIGHT-HEARTED It's important to avoid seriousness and stuffiness here. These colours need to be light, bright and give airiness and freshness to a space. I can't help but think of daffodil yellow or softer pinks, blues and greens in front of a backdrop of crisp white.

CURIOUS Exploration, requiring wisdom and also full of energy. The colours here jump around and move up and down the scale and are modern. I think of black to pink, warming olive green to vibrant orange, deep plum to cheery yellow, International Klein Blue to comforting coffee, icy blue to antique white or concrete grey to lipstick red.

VOICES

MATALI CRASSET, DESIGNER
Belleville, Paris, France

'When we are small, we like certain colours, but our preferences constantly change throughout our lives. People tend to play it safe and miss out on the incredible possibilities that colour could bring into their life. Colour is a universal language. When it is utilised well in a space or a product it can help with people's instinctive interaction about how the space or product should be used. We are still only scratching the surface in our understanding of the power of colour. We are yet to discover its full potential in how it affects our mental state and wellbeing.'

BUILDING HIGHLIGHT
A converted printing factory, now a home and studio. Every corner in the home has been used as a colour laboratory, exploring hues from plum and red to lime, yellow and crisp white.

BELIEF
When choosing colour, it's not scientific, it's a feeling. So many people are too conservative when it comes to colour.

LESSON
Colour is a designer's ally. It allows us to break codes and clarify proposed scenarios within a space.

'I refuse to be stuck in a box. When I choose a colour it plays a vital part in the overall function of the design's purpose.' — Matali Crasset

II

43

Communal
living

NO MAN IS AN ISLAND, ENTIRE OF ITSELF; EVERY MAN IS A PIECE OF THE CONTINENT, A PART OF THE MAIN.

John Donne, *Meditation XVII*, 1623

Feel connected

Amanda on
living together,
social design
& the need to belong

For too long now we have been living in a society that values individualism at the expense of community. However, quite simply, humans need to belong. Our basic psychological urge is to feel closely connected to others. We want to be part of a group and to fit in. We desire to be cared for and wish to avoid rejection. Wanting to 'belong' is what drives many of our feelings, thoughts and actions. In order to have happy, healthy lives we need to live together and support each other.

The home of London-based designer Lee Broom has been designed to be the perfect entertaining space. It feels open and glamorous, yet still provides a sense of privacy.

Communal living

In developed societies we might have become richer, but we are no happier. This may be due to the fact that, over time, we have been drifting apart from one another. Individuals and communities have become more independent, and our practical needs for one another have declined. While once whole villages would pitch in to help build a neighbour's home, now we would be lucky to know our neighbour's name. Many people live alone and many also work from home, and we spend much of our time shopping or socialising online rather than in person.

The home of Morten Bo Jensen, head designer of Vipp, features a kitchen designed to encourage people to stay and hang out, rather than just use the room for cooking.

In 1938 the Harvard Grant Study began examining qualities of wellness among people. It's still the most thorough study of wellbeing to date, with 268 men being observed over eight decades of their lives. The research was incredibly in-depth. The findings showed that the only thing that really matters in life is your relationships with other people.

The simple fact is that people who have more links with friends and family tend to be happier in all circumstances. This surely means that, when we are designing a home or developing residential buildings, the first thought should be, 'How can I design a space that creates togetherness, connection, a sense of belonging, and activates deep meaningful conversations?'

Many people today are concerned about the breakdown of the 'family unit'. Of course, the traditional idea of this has changed somewhat over time. The two-parent family home has evolved, and now we have single-parent families, multigenerational families and various kinds of blended families. These 'primary groups' orient our life. They give us a strong sense of who we are, our values and our beliefs at the most fundamental level. However, no matter what type of 'family' lives in a home, the same problems apply to all.

The common household is likely to have family members who are tucked away in different areas of the home – kids glued to television screens and parents on iPads, in the kitchen, catching up on housework or blogging on the computer upstairs. In the Happy Poll, 18 per cent of people said their family members were very likely to sit in different areas of the house when home at the same time and 36 per cent said this would happen sometimes. Only 52 per cent of people rated the quality of conversations between all members in the family to be above average.

Sadly, 17 per cent of people said that they felt lonely. About 17 per cent were feeling lonely as a result of not being able to share in deep and meaningful conversations, and 20 per cent felt they didn't have enough time to spend with family and friends. It was also common for single people, who were longing for an intimate relationship, to feel lonely.

When designing, always think about how you can add enjoyment for those who use the space and make them smile.

Don't get me wrong, loneliness and being alone are different things. Solitude can be lovely but, since the beginning of time, we have depended on each other for our survival. Not only did we hunt and gather food together, we provided safety, warmth and companionship for each other. We have evolved, but our instinct for wanting to 'belong' has remained constant.

German architect Anja Thede demonstrates that curtains are a great source of privacy in small, open spaces.

As cities get bigger and buildings higher, people are becoming more disconnected with one another. We need to find solutions to build trust and a strong sense of community.

COMMUNAL LIVING Agenda

'What makes my partner and I happy is entertaining at our home. We designed it to be theatrical, fun and full of surprises. We have had some great parties here that will remain wonderful memories for us and our friends for a very long time.' — Lee Broom, designer

Will the internet cause human extinction?

Despite social media and mobile phones, people under the age of 35 are feeling more alone than ever. Sociologist Eric Klinenberg of New York University says, 'it's the quality not the quantity of social interaction that best predicts loneliness'. We find sites like Facebook impersonal, distorting who our 'real' friends are and, rather than interacting in proper conversations, we become voyeurs who are happier to simply hit a 'like' button.

As social media reshapes how we connect, we need to rethink how we can be fulfilled in our relationships, and realise that no amount of tweets, texts or status updates can provide this. Instagram, Twitter and Facebook pale into insignificance when compared with a real, face-to-face conversation. Sharing a home means nothing if the only place you talk to people is on social media networks.

The average time people are spending on social media is alarmingly high. From the Happy Poll it is interesting to see how we are becoming addicted to it. Around 58 per cent said they do not feel better about their life after spending time on social media sites. A whopping 51 per cent said they actually felt worse. And it's not surprising to see that 56 per cent found the number of 'likes' on one of their social media posts could change their mood or self-esteem. As society continues to embrace technology and use it as a method of communication and interaction, it becomes more important to redevelop face-to-face social skills. The best place to start this development is at home.

Friends for life

The Japanese word *ikigai* roughly translates as 'that which makes one's life worth living'. The Japanese island of Okinawa is famous for having the oldest population in the world. Some think the key to the residents' long and healthy life is diet, but what most locals believe is that it's due to their strong connection with family and community. The elderly socialise with the young, and every Friday different villages on the island play host to other communities, giving the opportunity for residents to meet new faces or catch up with old friends and relatives.

It seems that having many strong social ties could help you live a longer and healthier life. According to a study from Brigham Young University and the University of North Carolina, 'individuals with adequate social relationships have a 50 per cent greater likelihood of longevity compared to those with poor or insufficient social relationships'.

Did you know that good conversations and even just listening to those you are interacting with can boost your brain power? Experts now believe that socialising, like other forms of mental exercise such as crossword puzzles, may build cognitive reserve – a reservoir of brain function you draw from if other areas of your brain begin to decline.

All this might sound rather depressing but, now we know what we are facing, we can empower ourselves and use this knowledge to design homes and spaces that will help to deliver happiness to the people in them, with design ideas that bring people together to talk and interact.

Open-plan living

'Open-plan' design means that all the rooms are visible, rather than being closed off behind walls. This kind of design encourages interaction between the members of the household and creates a sense of togetherness.

If you are not convinced about open plan, in the Happy Poll I found it fascinating that 81 per cent of people didn't feel the need for more privacy in the home. Sure, there are times when we all want a little 'me' time but, at the end of the day, people generally love to spend time with family or housemates. When we live in a place with others, we tend to want to spend time with them.

The key to successful open-plan living is focusing on having one, preferably big, social space where you can interact – but one that also provides a degree of privacy, so everyone can do their own thing while still feeling part of what's going on. What we are seeing more of in home design is a space where, no matter what floor you are on, it's possible to at least see, if not interact with, family members in other areas of the house.

Communal spaces need to be 'hot zones' that tempt family and friends to certain areas of the home, inviting them to linger, talk, play or be creative. The trick is to include alcoves, window seats, room dividers, curtains or interior windows, instead of walls and separate zones of furniture. A recessed seating area can look very dramatic and entice people to congregate there. The sunken living room, often referred to as the 'conversation pit', as part of a large, open living space creates a strong sense of intimacy. Designing separate levels within an open plan creates separate zones that offer both intimacy and privacy.

Change the dynamics

As the saying goes, 'the kitchen is the heart of the home'. I think we should look for clues in this wonderful room. People love to be around food and productivity. It sets the perfect scene to talk, laugh and share in some gossip.

I think we focus on the wrong spaces when we are creating comfort. We spend so much energy and money on our living rooms but, on average, most people only spend one to two hours a day there. In the Happy Poll, 70 per cent of people were willing to spend AUD $2000–$6000 on a sofa for the living room. But, for the dining table, 61 per cent of people were willing to spend only $700–$1000. If we invested in dining chairs, benches and stools that fulfilled the comfort required from a sofa, would we stay together in the kitchen longer? Why not experiment and opt for seating that is padded and preferably has a back?

If we didn't put so much emphasis on a comfy sofa in front of the television, we could create a more dynamic environment that would encourage people to sit around a table and talk. Imagine if you moved your sofa to be the main seating around the dining table, and your dining chairs went into the living room for watching the television – how your habits in the home would change!

Would it be so radical to give most of the living space over to the kitchen? The kitchen doesn't need to be only a functional space, often stark white, minimal and utilitarian. It should be a space that is designed to be warm, tactile, comfortable and tempting – the perfect place to bring people together.

To encourage those you love to stay longer around the feasting table, invest in comfortable seating. Make sure the benches have cushions.

The feasting table

I have been thinking for some time now how outdated the terms 'dining table' and 'dining room' are. They conjure up images of cold formality, stiff conversations, uncomfortable seating and a place that is only used occasionally.

We should swap the word 'dining' for something warmer like 'feasting'. If you said 'feasting table' and 'feasting room' you would instantly think of generosity, comfort and conversation flowing as quickly as the wine.

At special end-of-year holiday dinners or feasts, family and friends usually come together around a big table to catch up over the year's events and tell bad jokes and stories. It's hardly surprising, then, that a study from the London School of Economics showed that people are at their happiest when gathered around the holiday dinner table. I would love us to put the rituals and effort we invest into these feasts into our everyday living – but obviously without the extreme eating!

There is something wonderful about sharing a meal with family and friends. It doesn't matter if it's just a pizza. The National Center on Addiction and Substance Abuse at Columbia University has reported that children benefit from sharing regular meals with parents, from learning the importance of vegetables, how to use 'big words' and knowing which cutlery to use, to being less likely to smoke and drink, develop eating disorders or become depressed. And you might want to try to keep technology out of the mix. Only 29 per cent of people in the Happy Poll said that when they eat meals at home they make it a technology and television-free time.

In my opinion, the feasting table should be one of the largest pieces of furniture in the home. If it is big enough you can fill it up with friends and family, but it can also be a great place to work or study from. On a long table, two people can work at different ends – they have enough space between them to concentrate, but can still look up and see one another.

A round or long feasting table should always have stacked glasses, carafes of water, a bowl of nuts or fruit, salt, pepper, sugar and candles displayed casually in the centre, even when it's not being used. It makes the table welcoming and friendly and not intimidating.

Ritual ideas for your family & friends

To counteract 'human drift' we need to make time every day to connect with the important people in our life. Establish some weekly or other regular rituals to encourage this. Family rituals are habits or actions that are repeated periodically over time. They become something the family or household looks forward to. Every family should have their own rituals, as these become the foundation on which memories are created. Some ideas are:

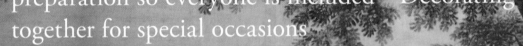

Dedicated movie night • Sunday roast meal around the 'feasting' table • Pizza Friday • Celebratory breakfast when someone receives good news • Walking the dog • Planting a flower or tree when someone in the household feels sad • Sunday gardening • Games night • Giving each family member a job in meal preparation so everyone is included • Decorating the home together for special occasions

Do nothing – together

IKEA's 2010 'Play Report', one of the largest studies ever conducted on family life, child development and the importance of play, found that 45 per cent of parents felt they didn't spend enough quality time with their children. Around 71 per cent of parents wanted to have more time to just chill out with their kids. Not doing anything special counted, as long as it was together. The report also showed that 53 per cent of children wanted to spend time in the kitchen with their mum and dad.

From impromptu dance parties to sorting socks, children just want to hang out more with parents, family and friends. What might seem like doing nothing is often the most rewarding activity; for example, just lying on the sofa talking. There is no rulebook about spending time together. Sometimes the best moments are unplanned, when everybody's in one place but not doing anything special. Make spaces in your home where you can just hang out, such as pillow-filled corners, big sofas and long tables. A home that is organised yet relaxed, functional yet comfortable, unfussy but also beautiful, can only help unite a family. The question is how do we do this? In this fast-paced technological world, when it comes to creating common areas, going back to basics is the most obvious solution.

Vertical living

You have probably noticed in your local cities that high-rise apartment blocks are popping up everywhere. Architects have tagged life in residential skyscrapers as 'vertical living'. With the cost of housing in major cities across the globe, people are forgoing the traditional backyard for tight living spaces in inner-city suburbs. It's important for people in these types of dwellings to feel connected with each other in order to increase their levels of happiness. However, there's evidence that high-rise life increases isolation and loneliness. People in these residential buildings (more than five floors) report a greater level of loneliness and have a harder time making new friends.

What many of our buildings are lacking is a sense of community. High-rise buildings need to focus on creating villages or suburbs within the development. They need to engage residents to talk and socialise with one another. The likelihood is that there are people living in the same building who have plenty in common.

Governments should ensure that apartment blocks have purposeful communal areas. These can be as simple as a shared library, a communal office space for residents to use when working from home, or an outdoor garden. These would also help to create a sense of community within a building, making the residents feel less isolated.

Social design

There has been an explosion of interest in the social design movement, which looks at how design can help build a better society, enabling people to live more productive, more fulfilled and therefore happier lives.

Excitingly, we are seeing urban designers tackle happiness in a strategic way. In Sydney, Australia, a building called Common Ground, owned by the charitable organisation Mission Australia, has been helping people come out of extreme homelessness and integrate back into society by providing them with permanent accommodation. There is a lot about the building that hasn't been executed to its best potential, but what is impressive is the social design that is evident. The residential building has been designed to accommodate a concierge as well as an on-site doctor, dentist, psychiatrist, gym, computer area, book swap area, television room and a communal kitchen where cooking classes are held. Pets are also allowed in the building. In my opinion a no-pet building is as bad as a sign saying 'no children allowed'. A pet is one of the best ways to get neighbours talking to each other, while providing company for the residents.

A lot of these ideas will become more apparent in residential apartment blocks in the future. A building will no longer be sold based on just location and aesthetics, but on how good the social design is. We are even seeing buildings introducing car-, bicycle- and tool-sharing services. Gallery spaces are also starting to pop up in vertical buildings, where residents can hold local art shows. We are seeing other buildings creating co-ops selling fresh produce grown on the rooftop, not only to people in the building, but also to the local community.

I'm confident we will see initiatives take place, such as including a restaurant in a residential building or a nearby restaurant offering room service. And it won't just be takeaway pizzas, fried chicken or nachos for dinner. Meals will be served on a beautiful plate that you leave outside your door when you are done, just as you do in a hotel.

Concierges will become more common, too. A concierge service tends to attract more owner–occupiers to residential buildings. I have lived in a couple of buildings with concierges, and I believe this service is not a luxury but a necessity for any city residential vertical building. This service is for far more than receiving deliveries. The concierge is a face you see every day, whom you can say hello to and shoot the breeze with, and residents can go to the concierge to sort problems with their apartments or neighbours. I can't tell you the difference it makes to have a concierge service.

However, you can't force interaction. I have seen too many examples of shared gardens, piazzas and common living spaces that don't engage people to use them. It's so important for a community, or group of people using shared spaces, to have input before the space is designed for them. There is no use having a library of books in a communal area if none of the residents read, or to have a shared edible garden if residents are not interested in putting the time in to care for it. If people are consulted from the beginning and actively help create the communal areas, they are more likely to have a sense of pride and ownership of the space. Plus it is a fantastic way to break the ice, allowing people to get to know their neighbours and form common bonds.

VOICES

HIROYUKI SHINOZAKI, ARCHITECT
Tokyo, Japan

Although at first glance the house looks like an open space with little privacy, the Terado family find alone time by having five floors over a traditional two-storey house. This gives an illusion of endless distance from each other through the height of the space. As the architect, Hiroyuki Shinozaki, says, 'We don't think connection itself is important, but we are interested in achieving changeable distance of space with those you share a space with. It's about the freedom of spending time with someone, or removing yourself from others, without feeling claustrophobic in a small area.'

BUILDING HIGHLIGHT

A narrow plot, 9.4 m (30 ft) high, designed to be private in a high-density neighbourhood. Inside, all the rooms over five floors, on all levels, are open and visually connected.

BELIEF

You don't have to include doors and walls in order to create privacy. It's about creating illusions of distance.

LESSON

It's possible to have an open house with a small footprint and yet still create privacy for those who live inside.

'We are often asked why Japanese houses are so open. We are looking for the subtle difference of distance, of spaces not being open or closed.'
— Hiroyuki Shinozaki

Downtime

THE TIME TO RELAX IS WHEN YOU DON'T HAVE TIME FOR IT.

Sydney J. Harris, *Strictly Personal*, 1953

Take a break

Amanda on
the cult of busy-ness,
our need to slow down
& the home as sanctuary

One of the biggest problems I have encountered in this study is that everyone is just 'too busy'. Most of us are putting more into our schedules than we can handle. Just this week I broke out in a rash, my hair was moulting like a labrador's and breathing calmly was becoming a problem – all the while my phone kept pinging with emails from people asking me to do this and that, and I was rushing from here to there. There were times I wanted to crawl into a little cave and hide from it all. But that would be stressful in itself because I would feel I was letting people down!

It's a brave new world for those who dare say they aren't busy. Watch out if you do! Is it just me feeling like I can't go a week without hearing how frantic others are? Sometimes it seems more like a competition than a plea for help. Being 'too busy' is like a badge of honour. In the Happy Poll, sadly 37 per cent of people believed they had to

A fireplace provides warmth and brings people together. It has the power to make us contemplate life with the meditative sounds of the roaring and crackling flames.

be busy, or appear to be busy to others, to prove they were successful. This is wrong and we should never have to feel guilty about taking time out for soul-nourishing activities.

Mixing warm and cool colours in a bedroom can be the perfect recipe for a good night's rest.

It seems we have lost our way in what we think success is. Shouldn't it be about doing less, being able to disconnect from work and stress, having the luxury to spend more time with family, going away on holiday or travelling, rather than being a hamster in a wheel? Surely, if you are successful you wouldn't be on the same crazy treadmill with the rest of us. I can't help but think of Richard Branson working from a hammock on his remote island. He's got the right idea!

We are living in an age of wealth and free-dom yet, overall, society is experiencing an epidemic of despondency and depression. Many people are working themselves into the ground in the pursuit of making money, in order to chase fleeting pleasures in what is our shrinking free time. However, money doesn't buy happiness – countless studies have proven that. This way of living can be harmful. In Japan they call it *karoshi*, which means 'death by overworking'. According to the Japanese Ministry of Health, Labour and Welfare, 'sudden deaths of any employee who works an average of 65 hours per week or more for more than 4 weeks, or on average 60 hours or more per week for more than 8 weeks, may be *karoshi*'. Our notion of success and luxury has been turned on its head. It isn't bling most of us are after these days, just peace and quiet.

Although we are constantly being told, 'Slow down, stop, take a breather', how do we put the brakes on and enjoy life? Most of us hate to be told to slow down, so the trick is to create a space in your home that makes you want to.

In today's fast-paced world, we welcome a place to chill out, to release stress and recharge. Unfortunately, the modern world isn't geared up for us to embrace the words 'slow', 'relax' or 'downtime', and most houses today are designed to be convenient to help us keep on track with our busy schedules. To achieve serenity, a home needs to harmonise with its surroundings, while creating a womb-like sense of security and peace.

This idea of the home being a sanctuary or an escape is nothing new. Home is meant to be the place we find solitude, relaxation and stillness. However, in reality, home is your family's HQ, nursery and canteen, and maybe even your workplace. The minute you walk into the house, you will feel like there is so much to do – school lunches, dinner, cleaning, washing, homework. Chores will always be there. We need a home design that can make these things easier to do and not be so time-consuming.

Cosy corners filled with slubby cushions made from natural fibres help you to unwind and enjoy your home.

When asking people about what makes them happy they often say it's the small things in life. But we need downtime to be able to enjoy them. This is where design can play such an important role in creating spaces that tempt and convince us to slow down and simply savour the good things around us. I always fall back onto five words when beginning the design process for shared spaces: Privacy. Entertainment. Ambience. Comfort. Ergonomics. (PEACE). They're good words to remember when designing!

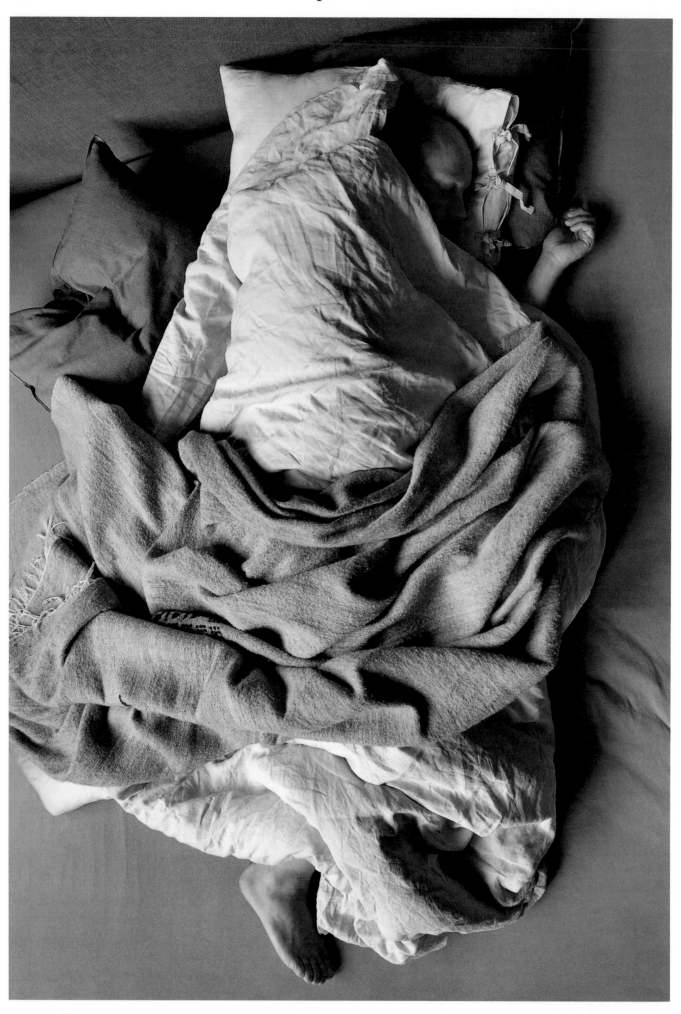

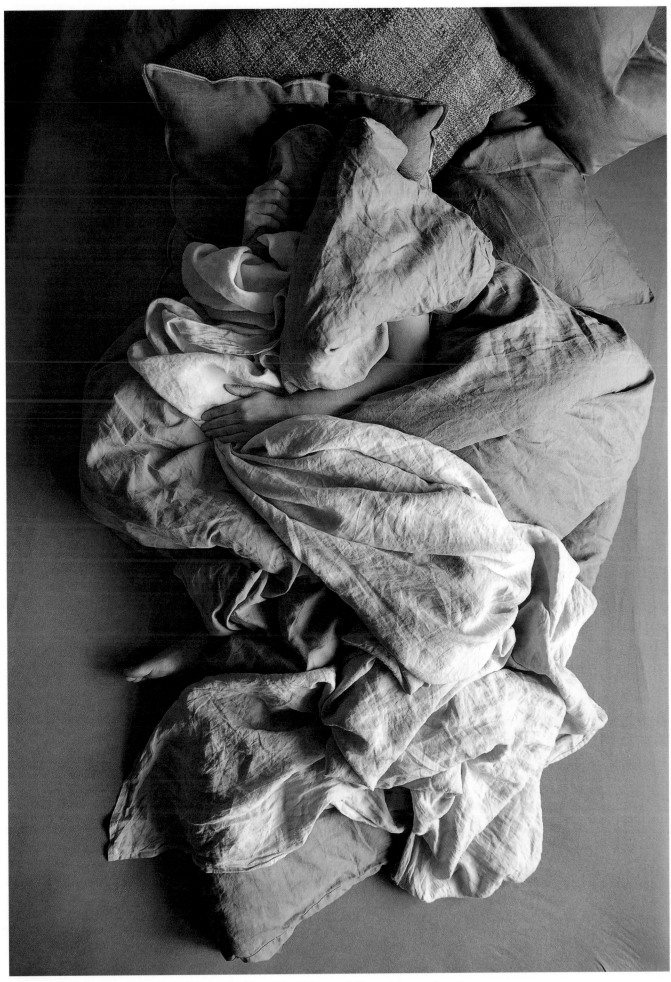

I guarantee that linen sheets will help you sleep better because they feel so good. They will be one of your best investments.

We all need quiet times, not only to read but to have moments to re-evaluate our week, our lives and our future. We need these 'shhh' times to recharge so we can be our best selves.

DOWNTIME
Agenda

Turn the TV off!

The slow movement

The relaxation effect

A good night's sleep

Cosy and comfortable

Getting some shhh time

Turn the TV off!

Did you know that watching TV can make you sad? The average person watches more than four hours of television a day, yet research clearly shows it doesn't make us feel any happier.

I love watching rubbish television. Telling you is like admitting my dirty little secret, especially to those who don't have a television at home. Yes, I love watching soaps. I know, I know. Sadly, my fellow television watchers, I don't bear good news. The most commonly reported emotion when watching our favourite shows on television is depression. A study showed that watching a lot of television vastly increases our desire for more possessions and every hour we watch reduces our contentment by 5 per cent.

Believe me, it's not easy to quit when you live with a household of people who love watching TV. It's likely that everyone will want to watch different shows on different nights. But try to make a pact that you will only watch the TV three nights a week. Then try to gradually reduce the viewing time even more over the next six months.

There is good news, though. It seems that watching uplifting movies can dramatically alter your mood for the better. Several studies have shown that watching funny and inspirational films is a very effective way to temporarily improve our spirits. Therefore maybe we need to ditch the idea of the television room and concentrate on creating a stimulating home cinema room. Rather than being an occasional pleasure, regularly watching movies can become

a powerful mood lifter. A warning though, depressing and violent films will obviously invoke the opposite feelings.

If you are filling your evenings with Twitter, Instagram, Facebook, blogging, television, checking emails – more than likely simultaneously – please just STOP! You are winding your brain up with way too much digital input to relax. This is preventing your brain from releasing the necessary natural sleep chemicals for you to rest and repair your mind and body overnight. You don't have to switch the devices off all evening – although that would be good – but at least give yourself two hours' digital-free time before bed. Philosopher Alain de Botton recommends the 'news Sabbath', which begins late on Friday evening and continues till Sunday evening. During that time we are encouraged to not go anywhere near a news source and to resist the impulse to check phones. Instead, we should experience the world firmly through our own eyes.

Try to relax – read, walk your dog after dinner, listen to music and have conversations with friends and loved ones. The likelihood is you will sleep better and feel more refreshed and energised for the next day, be way more productive, and you will actually have time to breathe. It sounds so easy but we still never seem to do these things. Take my advice, try it for just one week to see the results and you will swear by it.

Emma Persson Lagerberg and Bengt Lagerberg (drummer with the band The Cardigans), have created their downtime space with the things they love.

Emma Persson Lagerberg and Bengt Lagerberg enjoy their 'holy Friday' – their Friday evening is all about spending time only with family.

The slow movement

The terms FOMO (fear of missing out) and YOLO (you only live once) have become recent mottos, creating extra pressure on us to fit more into our life. However, maybe there is a different pace at which to live?

The Slow Movement was created as a backlash against modern life's fast pace. Initially, it focused on food, and the Slow Food organisation was born to counteract the world's obsession with fast food. Similarly, Slow Design is concerned with the long-term wellbeing of humans and the natural environment. Creatives in this movement are concerned with sustainable designs and focusing on nonmaterial things, including experiences, and they try to take human behaviour and natural time cycles into account when designing buildings.

Slow Design defiantly celebrates the ritual of 'making', and reminds us of the way people used to do things. For example, in recent years there has been a movement away from the quick-fix espresso machines back to the classic, beautifully crafted, pour-over coffee makers. More effort is required to use them, but the whole process is slower, more authentic, sensual and almost meditative. Many of us enjoy food and drink more when we know it has been lovingly prepared – for example slow-cooked casseroles or home-brewed beer. We will pay a little extra for a cushion if it has been screen-printed rather than digitally produced, or a chunky throw knitted by a local artisan, rather than bought off the rack from a chain store.

It is looking pretty clear that our modern world's addiction to speed is eroding our productivity and health as well as our quality of life, so I feel we should be embracing the principles of Slow Design.

Why not try a bit of slow living? Make a list of what you do in a week, from most to least important. You are probably trying to fit in too many things. If you want to slow down, you need to do less. See if you can cut out some of the less important tasks from the bottom of your list, then maybe you could instead try to grab yourself some downtime, where you switch off your phone, find a comfortable place and simply reflect and recharge for 20 minutes. You can also prevent rushing by scheduling more time between meetings or appointments. Or perhaps try some slow rituals, such as gardening, meditation, yoga or tai chi.

Just stop and look around you. Spend at least half an hour talking to your child, partner or a friend; look at the sky and notice the movements the wind makes; listen to birds singing; read a book or have a long, luxurious bath. When was the last time you stopped and enjoyed a painting or photo you have hanging in your home? When was the last time you sat on a comfy couch and just daydreamed for half an hour? Daydreaming isn't a waste of time. In fact it's been shown to have positive effects. A study from the University of California has found that people who daydream may be more effective problem solvers. It's important to create buildings and homes to encourage those inside to daydream – a window to look out of, a hidden room, or photos that stimulate memories of a place or time, are all things you should consider when designing.

Julie Vandenbroucke commissioned architects 51n4e and textile designer Chevalier-Masson to create a daybed to encourage people to socialise and relax.

The relaxation effect

During my research for this book I made some big changes in my own
life that I hoped would help me find a better work–life balance and,
well, just make me happier. It wasn't as easy as I thought.

Some things, like adding new colour in my home and
changing the type of bed linen I use, have been the easier,
happier challenges. One of the areas I struggled with, though,
was embracing yoga and meditation.

I booked a few times to learn to meditate. I don't know
why, but I was so nervous. My cynical nature kicked in when
I found out it would cost me big bucks. I really struggled to
find a type of yoga or meditation that worked for me. I knew
I had to push through the doubt and commit, because so much
research has proven both yoga and meditation help us unplug,
de-stress and centre ourselves, and make us happier. I had to
discover why all roads to happiness seemed to keep coming
back to this place. What I learnt was that relaxing with a cup of
tea or lounging on the sofa isn't enough. We need to experience
deep relaxation, where tension is released from the body on
a physical level and your mind completely switches off.

Don't worry, I'm not convincing you to become a
Buddhist and chant, but you should know that just 20 minutes
of meditation a day is said to be the equivalent of two to three
hours' rest a day. This all helps with clarity, focus and increased
energy. It can train our brains to increase self-esteem and
improve memory, intelligence and creativity – some say it can
help depression, skin disorders, anxiety, substance abuse and,
of course, it has a positive effect on our happiness levels.

The more of us who commit to these techniques,
the more important it is to create spaces in buildings that give
people the confidence and silence to practise relaxation
techniques. If you are like me, you probably hardly have room
for an extra chair, let alone a full meditation or yoga room. But
just a small nook in your home might be something you could
repurpose space to create. You need a quiet place, so why not
put a favourite chair in an area of the home that is hardly used,
or shut the bedroom door and sit on your bed? However, if
you are lucky enough to have a spare room to transform, here
are some valuable tips.

First, you want the room to be a place where you feel
relaxed as soon as you enter it. Choose colours that you find
calming – blues, greens and yellows in soft natural tones are
pretty safe. Stay away from red or orange. Make sure the
lighting can be dimmed if it comes from overhead, or use
candles or lamps instead for a more ambient effect. Some
people like to include small Japanese fountains, as they find
the water sounds help with relaxation. Most importantly,
make sure you keep phones, TVs and computers out of the
room – but you might want to include a sound system to play
soft music. You could also display some beautiful items and
ornaments that you find calming, but don't fill the room with
clutter. Unless something is going to help you relax, leave it out.

A good night's sleep

Our days are filled with so much activity, it's a wonder we sleep at all! With the rise of anxiety, depression and insomnia and increasingly long working hours, a deep, restful night's sleep has never been more important.

Apart from the sobering idea that not getting enough sleep may be linked to an increased risk of disease, studies show that a good night's sleep is linked to happiness. Yet, I have noticed over the years that the bedroom is one of the most overlooked rooms when it comes to decorating, as we tend to concentrate on the public areas of the home. However, creating a calming, soothing, sound- and light-proof, relaxing environment in your bedroom should be your top priority! If you get it right it can have a major impact on the quantity and quality of sleep you will get. If you regularly have a healthy night's sleep you are more likely to have a positive outlook on life. A study has even shown that an extra hour's sleep every night can do more for happiness than a substantial raise in pay! Let's face it, when we miss out on a night of sound sleep it's much harder to stay patient with your partner or the kids, especially when you are trying to get them off to school.

It's no accident that you often sleep better when you stay in hotels. Hotel chains know that good linen and beds are the guarantee to repeat business. We should treat the bed at home with the same level of attention. This is where we relax, nap, sleep, make love and maybe even work, watch television, eat and drink. As research involving 45,000 Apple smartphone users claims that sex boosts our mood more than anything else, this is reason enough for having a comfortable bed! Always buy the best-quality bed, mattress and bedding you can afford, and replace your mattress every five to seven years. For a good night's sleep, couples should opt for a queen- or king-sized bed.

The Happy Poll found that 30 per cent of people were spending, on average, AUD $3000 for their mattress. Am I alone in thinking that investing in a super-comfortable mattress is pointless if you're going to ruin the effect with stiff, hospital-corner bed linen? Instead, adopt loosely layered sheets, bedspreads and blankets, allowing ends to drape casually on the floor to create a far more relaxed and inviting mood. Choose sensual fabrics that feel good against the skin, such as cool cotton and linen for sheets, luscious velvets and soft wool for blankets and covers and quilts that are silky and smooth. Bedroom rugs should be made from tactile materials that feel great underfoot.

Bedrooms should be cool, quiet and dark. Temperature is important and, if you are too hot or cold, it might be affecting your sleep. Memory foam pillows might be all the rage, but they can get very hot. Candles or lamps with low-wattage bulbs are preferable to a bright overhead light. Sunlight is a natural, positive source of energy during the day, but it can disrupt deep, restful sleep. The rising sun is the cue for the brain to wake up, so keep it out of the room while you sleep. Your bedroom should feel soothing, sensual and restful, so use shades of colour that are associated with sunset. Think greens, lavender, mauves and caramel.

During the night, even if you are not looking at your phone, each time you get a message, it pings, vibrates and lights up the room. So, before you go to bed, leave your devices in another room. Get a traditional alarm clock instead.

'A nook on a window ledge is a perfect place to sit, read and daydream.' — Chloe Macintosh, creative director

Cosy and comfortable

In Denmark, which was recently ranked the happiest country in the world, they conclude that happiness in the home is achieved by something called *hygge*. This word doesn't translate well but, basically, *hygge* is all about comfort and being surrounded by familiar and cosy things. Comfort helps ease our time in a space and gives us freedom without restraint.

Casual comfort is the Holy Grail of design, when you want to get friends and family to spend more time in one spot. Although we want our homes to look stylish, we like them to be cosy and relaxed too. Achieving this delicate balance between the informal and chic can be difficult. If a trendy chair, sofa or room isn't comfortable, it is essentially useless. My advice is to surround yourself with tons of texture. Surfaces that treat the fingers and thrill the toes instantly instil the desired degree of laid-back luxe. A basic sofa can be completely transformed with piles of colour-coordinated slubby wool cushions and a few sheepskin throws, just as any floor is invigorated with an impromptu patchwork of rugs (to use one is simply not enough – think Berber tent-style), and a bed is not dressed in my opinion until it has been layered with linens, a quilt and a couple of silky or chunky throws.

Setting the right ambience in a room is everything. Will your family and friends be more likely to come together when a space is intimate and cosy? Or would they prefer open spaces filled with natural daylight? When you work out what they prefer, you need to embrace it and take the theme all the way. Half-hearted and confused messages in a design tend to unsettle people, as can uncomfortable seating, jarring colours, overbright lighting and extremes of heat or cold.

Getting some shhh time

It's important to free yourself and get away from the hassles of work, the nagging at home and the pressures you face daily. It's okay to run away and break out from it all, but you don't have to spend a fortune on holidays or yoga retreats. All you need is to find your own corner in the home – a place you can flee to and have some shhh time.

For our wellbeing we need to turn off the television, step away from the computer, flick on some music, read or just sit quietly and let our mind have some time to take us on a journey. People all around the world have found their tranquil corner at home by creating alcoves, using curtains, screens or silent pods, or going into the bathroom or bedroom to have some alone time.

Interestingly, in the Happy Poll, 81 per cent of people felt they had enough privacy at home. Size of family and space doesn't seem to have challenged people in the need for privacy. I guess it's no surprise we like, and often love, the people we live with, so we enjoy the time we have with them. However, sometimes we all want to do different activities in the home, so we need to be able to close a door or slide a curtain across to have some privacy.

And it's not just adults who need to find quiet time. There is a library full of books with titles such as *The Over-scheduled Child* or *The Pressured Child*, and parents are filling their child's every hour with sports, music lessons, homework and play dates, leading to an increase in children suffering from stress. Set up your home to work for your children. Create secret doors into a playroom, provide them with their own chair or sofa to hang out on, have lots of floor cushions or a rug for them to draw or read on. Help them in designing their bedroom to be a place where they can daydream and imagine other worlds.

Chapter Three

VOICES

MIRKO BEETSCHEN, JOURNALIST
& STÉPHANE HOULMAN, CREATIVE PLANNER
Interlaken, Switzerland

'You will only want to spend time at home if you love it. When I first stepped inside our home it embraced me and kissed me all over. To relax at home you need to ignore design stereotypes and do what you feel is right. Why not put carpets on your wall or hang a hammock? My favourite place to have a nap is on our linen sofa in our downstairs living room, surrounded by the rich original timber panelling and warming parquet floors. We like to use lots of table and floor lights to create an atmosphere of calmness and warmth. We use natural fabrics and materials with a mix of modern pieces of furniture, interspersed with antiques and vintage pieces. There are 40 different shades in the colour palette, ranging from the palest pearl grey to spearmint green, to reflect subtle mood variations.

'We cook, bake, make tea, sleep, talk, read, eat, drink and are mesmerised by the fire crackling in the fireplace. We go for walks and enjoy the mountain air when we are here. This is the place where we and our friends and family get a chance to stop and put things in our lives back into perspective. Anyone who walks through our door immediately drops their guard.'

BUILDING HIGHLIGHT

A 200-year-old farmhouse has been sympathetically converted into a modern home. Every wall has been painted in calming, soothing colours that will help to unwind the most stressed-out soul.

BELIEF

A home should not be just for the people who live there, but a place that everyone can enjoy and relax in and leave any stress outside. It should make people feel instantly comfortable and encourage them to be themselves.

LESSON

When you create a home that relaxes you, it's amazing how much more open you are to finding time to talk to your loved ones and neighbours, and enjoying the simple things in life.

'We found that dirty colours with a lot of grey in them soothe people and set the scene that this is a house to unwind in.' — Mirko Beetschen

Edit

EVERY INCREASED POSSESSION LOADS US WITH A NEW WEARINESS.

John Ruskin, *The Eagle's Nest*, 1872

Free yourself

Amanda on
having too much stuff,
considered simplicity
& buying less and feeling better

Editing is the skill of this century. When we have less stuff and less space we produce less carbon dioxide, have more dollars, and we are happier. We have a sense of freedom when we are less weighed down by excess belongings. Many of our homes are so choked with clutter, that we seem to be crowded out by furniture and possessions. Yet it's us – not the furniture and decoration – who should take centre stage. The home is a backdrop to our lives and not the other way round.

Edit

So often I hear people say, 'My house is too small' or 'There isn't enough storage'. However, it's likely that the problem is not with the size of the house or the amount of storage space, but with the amount of things that you have crammed into the house. You need to do some editing.

We tend to complicate our lives by spending too much money on items to fill our houses, whether we need them or not, from new furniture and this season's cushions, to the latest electronics. It has become a modern madness to pursue ever greater material wealth for no obvious purpose. But it's all a trap. Although 28 per cent of people in the Happy Poll said they have, at some time, purchased items for the home to make them feel happier, research shows that an obsession with material gain actually makes us less happy and, in one study, it was shown that material objects were nine times less important to people than nonmaterial things such as family and friends. So, rather than making you feel better, buying more stuff is probably causing you to feel more stressed and anxious.

Considered simplicity is not about creating minimalist perfection with no character – it's about removing the unwanted clutter that is annoying and ugly.

According to spiritualist Shaykh Fadhlalla Haeri, one of the essential keys to human happiness is a person's level of self-discipline. Regular overindulgence in alcohol, food or sex can tax and weaken the body, mind and soul. Getting out of control in our shopping habits and buying things that we don't need is also a problem. If we practise self-discipline in this area, not only will it be possible to enhance our self-image and cut back on the number of possessions we own, we will also become masters of our homes rather than slaves to it. Restraint leads to stability and stability to contentment. Ask yourself if your shopping habits are out of hand. If the answer is yes, you need to take stock.

If you do go for a minimalist look, choose sculptural items that add interest to a space.

I believe that when we feel we have lost our way or control, we need to stop and look back at where we started. For our ancient ancestors, belongings had much less importance. Life was tough. All energy was focused on survival – hunting and gathering. The home was a place to offer shelter and some degree of safety. The furniture was designed for robust function. It also needed to be mobile due to the nomadic lifestyle – boards of wood that rested on diners' laps served as tables and were hung on the wall to be kept out of the way when not in use. People lived only with what they needed to survive. It's over the centuries, as survival has become less physical and nomadic, that we have had time to add all the fluffy stuff that we don't need.

We all know less is more, but how much do you require to survive and live a happy life? It comes down to buying only what you really love and what you need. The 'edited' life is about making conscious decisions.

When we choose to have less, we shouldn't brand it as 'minimalism' but rather 'considered simplicity'. Minimalism evokes too many thoughts of cold, hard-edged, expensive rooms with no furniture in them. Considered simplicity is demonstrating that we are intelligently lightening the burden of our spaces. By owning less, worrying less and pushing ourselves less, we can restore a sense of balance in our life.

British designer Lee Broom displays a few of his most cherished items on his 'Heritage Boy' tile coffee table in his London home.

EDIT
Agenda

Will having more things make me happy?

Less is more

A lifetime of belongings

The quest for authenticity

Keep it real

Sustainability

Have a vision and stick to it

Assess your actual needs

Go digital

Remove the clutter

'I want our designs to embody beauty and history and, most importantly, outlive fleeting trends.' — Jonas Bjerre-Poulsen, architect

Will having more things make me happy?

People are constantly moaning, 'I wish I had…' or 'If only I had…' Our society and advertising are much to blame, as we are surrounded by messages telling us that our lives will improve if only we bought more stuff. On average, we see 3500 advertising messages every day. But we are wasting valuable energy. This constant coveting and dreaming about other people's possessions steals our joy and contentment. It makes us feel like we are missing out, even though there is often so much potential happiness right in front of us.

Like our bodies, we dress our homes to impress others. I know I'm not alone in thinking, 'How many more cushions do I need on our sofa?' or 'Will this new vase help my home to become magazine-worthy?' We have got things confused. The sofa is often one of the least used pieces of furniture in the home. Yet, because it's in a public part of the home, it's one of the biggest ticket items. However, people spend way less on a mattress, one of the most used objects in the home, as it is hidden away and covered with bedding. Why spend more than AUD $10,000 on an item we only use one to three hours a day, yet pay a fraction of this for something used more than eight hours a day? Or, to be more radical, why even have a major piece of furniture in your home at all if you use it less than an hour a day!

Less is more

Less is truly more, not only for the aesthetics of our homes but for our own mental wellbeing. Around 41 per cent of people from the Happy Poll said they feel burdened by having too many things in their home.

You can't buy happiness, so stop spending money on what you don't need. Before you make any new purchase, ask yourself these three questions:

- Will this item need to be replaced within two years?
- Is this item not worth its value to be repaired, reupholstered or reloved?
- Am I likely to throw this item on the street when I'm done with it, because it will have no worth?

If you answer yes to the above questions then my advice is don't buy it. You are just burning your money, so save for a little longer. If you wait, you can purchase something of real quality that you love and that will last. This is better, not only for the sake of your bank balance, but for your wellbeing and happiness, not to mention the environment.

A lifetime
of belongings

We have become shopaholics and, like any addict, we are hoarding our stash.
Shopping has become our vice. We know we don't need more stuff, but like
all addicts we come back for more.

Honestly, what are we doing? I was recently faced with a life lesson about what happens to all the stuff we spend our money on throughout our lives. My grandparents recently passed away and all their years of purchases ended up on the floor for the family to sift through to take what they wanted and leave what they didn't. Everyone mainly went for items that had strong memories associated with them. The rest of the goods went either to the garbage dump or a charity shop.

This process hit me really hard. I visualised all the material proof of my life's hard work, sacrificing of dreams, worry and stress about money eventually ending up on a floor somewhere one day. It became clear that the only things we leave that are of any real value are the memories, which are cherished by our family, friends and loved ones.

Don't burden your kids with your stuff. Don't worry that they will fight over your belongings when you go. And don't be so cocky as to think that when you make expensive investments you are creating family heirlooms. The likelihood is that your offspring will not share the same taste as you. Heirlooms are great if those who receive them don't feel a guilt-ridden obligation to take them off your hands and are forced to squeeze an eight-seater dining table into a small studio apartment. Make sure they will want it and love it, together with all its spots and blemishes.

Am I a hoarder?

1. Your belongings give you more discomfort than comfort
2. You have a fear of letting go of things
3. You commonly say, 'I need to hold onto this because you never know when I might need it again!'
4. You own more than one or two of the same object
5. You have a pewter cup full of old lottery tickets and pens that don't work
6. You have piles of faded paperwork, junk mail and old bills that will be read and filed one day
7. You hold on to discarded broken machines in case there is a fix for them one day
8. There are unopened boxes that haven't been touched for more than two years

The best advice I can give you is:
throw it all away!

Architect Jonas Bjerre-Poulsen has focused on simplicity, functionality and tactility in his family home just outside Copenhagen.

The quest for authenticity

We consumers are sick of being sold the same story. If you walk down a main street and look at what the homeware stores are selling, they're all stocking the same stuff. More of us are slowly waking up and asking where the 'authenticity' is in that. Where is the love? Where can I find something I want to keep? Isn't it astonishing that we have no knowledge of and, more damningly, no interest in finding out, the way many of the things we own were made, where they came from and who made them.

However, there is a movement bubbling, driven by shoppers searching for authenticity. We are so overwhelmed with products that if something stands out we tend to appreciate it and are willing to spend more on it. Big brands are gradually realising it isn't sustainable to pump out new products every week, so they are slowing down and starting to embrace the concept of handmade craftsmanship. Individuality is the antidote to mass consumption. We want the love, we want the handcrafted.

Some brands are recognising the importance of being authentic. Many Italian designer brands betrayed their DNA to cut costs and increase margins, by outsourcing production to Asia. However those same companies have recently moved production back to Italy. The 'Made in Italy' tag is a strong part of the brand story. We are not only buying the product, we are buying the story.

Keep it real

In the Happy Poll, 24 per cent said it was important for them to own designer furniture. This is fine, but 30 per cent of this group said they would buy a fake designer piece if they couldn't afford the original. Chief designer Morten Bo Jensen from Danish brand Vipp told me, 'Design is not just about aesthetics, it's the promise and story of the brand'. Buying fakes means people are buying into the idea of the kudos, trying to match a bourgeois lifestyle, rather than buying into the promises of the original pieces. To buy a fake is in a sense saying you are willing to live a fake life. The copy is not designed for its quality, craftsmanship, provenance, sustainability or its long-lasting value. Instead it may be poorly made with no apparent craftsmanship, is of unknown provenance and almost certainly will not keep its value.

My point is that if you buy these fakes you are setting the scene for someone's else's lifestyle, one you feel you have a right to but can't afford. That chair, table or light will always be fake, and for you to develop a deep love for this product is unlikely. You are missing the emotional purpose of the brand or design's promise. I have very little designer furniture in my home because I can't afford it. But when I do get a piece, it's a much-loved item. I suggest that you save a little longer and purchase an original, or get creative and look at other alternatives – buy vintage, reclaim/redesign an item you already own, discover young affordable designers or, better still, make or design your own.

Sustainability

Another driving factor for our future happiness is sustainability. We have become more aware of the need to help our planet as we hear the frightening statistics of waste involved in making our bargain-priced products. Cost and instant fashionable looks have become our priorities when consuming. We feel like we have come out with value if we can fill a shopping basket with clothes and accessories for a couple of hundred dollars, or if we can deck out our whole home in one go for less than a couple of thousand. It's false economy. We need to change this way of thinking – value comes not from the cheapest bargain price, but from well-made, long-lasting beauty.

You have the power to choose where you spend your dollars. If you slow down your spending and impulse-buying, you can invest the money saved in quality items that will last longer. We should reprogram ourselves to learn how to make considered purchases. We must learn value by identifying what we do need and what we don't. It's better to purchase objects that are well made and can be repaired and not simply thrown away when they break.

Have a vision and stick to it

Most people don't have any real long-term vision when designing their home. As a result, we often purchase things as quick fixes for obstacles that appear day to day. The problem with these short-term solutions is they often stick around for the long term and we find ourselves saying, 'It will be so much better when we get so and so'. Usually those temporary fixes eventually find themselves in landfill. Around 54 per cent of people from the Happy Poll said they regularly throw objects and furniture on the side of the road or give them to charity shops. Don't be surprised if, even though you have donated your goods to a charity, they still end up in landfill.

Having a future focus not only gives you a positive goal when you are implementing changes, it makes things more exciting and helps make short-term decorating problems more bearable. To experience a happier home, decide on a vision and work towards your long-term goal daily. See it clearly and believe it. Take action and make it a reality. Imagine your ideal life in your home for you and your family. When your vision is clear, it's so much easier to reject things in your home that don't fit into your long-term plan. It's almost impossible to feel depressed about your space if you have a motivating focus for the future, which you are working towards with hope and consistency.

'Don't forget to focus on the little details, from door handles to light switches.' — Michael Leeton, architect

'To preserve the spirit of a room is the challenge of change.' — Jan Rösler, architect

Assess your actual needs

Deciding what you really need requires taking a good long look at how you live your daily life, and prioritising the activities and items that are already a part of your lifestyle. When I talked to Swedish interiors journalist Emma Persson Lagerberg, she told me, 'I want to simplify my life. I want to feel lighter from the possessions that I have.'

It's time to ask some questions. Does anyone actually sit in the chair in the corner? How often do you eat at that table? When was the last time you used your iPod? Does anyone send you messages on your fax machine anymore? Do the chipped, novelty tea-stained mugs really have such an emotional hold on you? If the treadmill is gathering geological dust, perhaps a pair of trainers would be more useful and take up significantly less space?

Perhaps it's time for a big spring clean and for you to sift through your cabinets, closets and shelves. Only keep the things you can't live without. Immediately throw away any boxes filled with unimportant things that haven't seen the light of day for years. There is a reason why you haven't opened them. You don't need the stuff in them. Stop being illogically sentimental about your possessions.

Go digital

Technology can be an enormous help when it comes to editing. Instead of owning hundreds of books, magazines or newspapers, we can simply download them onto our electronic tablets or other devices. We can store our music and movies on our computers or even our phones, and many of us tap into online resources to listen to music or watch movies, negating the need for any bulky home storage. New photos are stored digitally and old family photos can be scanned and stored the same way. Most of us look up information on the internet, so we no longer need huge telephone directories, street directories, sets of encyclopedias or shelves of 'how-to' books.

Mirrors and windows are becoming 'smart', meaning our digital life can be viewed on them via technology. Our emails, social media, TV shows, movies and Skype chats can even be viewed on these devices. Therefore, the need to own DVD players, game consoles, televisions and their accessories is vanishing. However, it's important to stay in control of the technology, so that it's simplifying rather than complicating your life.

Remove the clutter

If the feeling of being out of control is utterly overwhelming you, it is possible to get things back on track. You will see immediate results by sorting out your clutter.

I have a knack for taking on more than my house can handle or, as I often say, 'spreading the house too thin'. It's not that I want my home to operate at such a high-stress level, it's just that I get excited about new objects and furniture and I can't wait to see things in my house.

There is one room I call my 'challenged space' – or you might consider it a scene of devastation – where I store my clothes and house the washing machine and dryer. There is so much going on in this room, that I literally feel paralysed every time I walk in there, wondering what I should do with the mess. When it comes to other people's stuff and how their space should work I'm a pro, but when organising my own, it sometimes feels like I'm clawing my way up Everest. It's one thing to tell people to throw their things out, but it's another throwing out your own. Plus, when you are telling family members to put their things away or do a chuck-out, usually voices rise, doors slam and resentment grows.

Clearing life of too much stuff will help give you back control over your environment. Take an inventory of where you are. Work from a list to help you keep focused.

Often, when decluttering, you will be overwhelmed by the size of the project. Break those big jobs down into several achievable portions to help manage your time more effectively. This will help to prevent that 'Where do I start?' feeling from sneaking in and slowing everything down.

Try these simplifiers to help you edit some things that might be burdening you at home:

- Throw out at least a third of your books, clothes and possessions that you no longer need.
- Rethink the furniture and objects you have in each room. Is each piece being used and is it overcrowding the space?
- Make sure 70 per cent of what you purchase for your home will at least retain its value, if not grow in value.
- One hundred per cent of your objects should have a regular use, function or a happy memory attached to them. If they don't, throw them out.
- Set a rule that if you bring one thing into your home, then one thing must go out.
- Aim to get at least one piece of furniture handmade for your home this year.

111

VOICES

ARNO BRANDLHUBER, ARCHITECT
Mitte district, Berlin, Germany

'We fill our homes with too much stuff that we don't need. I purchase most of my furniture on Ebay and, if I tire of it, I resell it for approximately the same price I paid for it. This is smart economy. Get more space – pay less. Also, don't spend too much money on a space. I always go for land and buildings that other people stay away from. I then like to work with the existing problems rather than fight against them.'

BUILDING HIGHLIGHT

With Brutalist concrete being the main backdrop for the home, this reduces the feeling of clutter in the design.

BELIEF

Good architecture can always be two things: good-looking and sustainably designed. Don't define a space to be something that cannot be changed.

LESSON

The happiest spaces are the ones that give complete flexibility in how someone wants to live. It's important for people to carve out their own needs and desires.

'I believe design should be lo-fi – by using raw concrete walls, plywood, iron pipes, polycarbonate boards. Editing materials in a building means you can produce more affordable but well-designed homes.' — Arno Brandlhuber

Flow

THE GRACE OF A CURVE IS AN INVITATION TO REMAIN. WE CANNOT BREAK AWAY FROM IT WITHOUT HOPING TO RETURN.

Gaston Bachelard, *The Poetics of Space*, 1958

Clear a path

Amanda on
flow states,
natural continuity
& intuitive design

You have probably heard of 'flow states'. Being in a flow state means that you are so focused on and engrossed in an activity, whether it be work or play, that your state of consciousness is altered. We are so intent on the task that we forget about the world around us and don't even notice the passing of time. Nothing else seems to matter while we are absorbed in the flow state. Hungarian psychologist Mihaly Csikszentmihalyi has studied happiness and creativity, and discovered that humans feel fulfilled and happy when they are in a flow state.

I don't think it's too big a jump to apply this theory to our homes, our buildings and city planning. We are constantly looking to solve problems, seeking out ways to add a positive force to people's everyday lives. When in well-designed spaces or when using thoughtfully created products, people may linger longer than they planned to because they are having fun, being productive, or both. When we experience joy or contentment with a space or product, the happier we are. If you create flow in a design, you are creating an optimal experience for those who use it.

When working out the floor layout of your furniture, make sure you create easy access flow in thoroughfares.

Flow

Successful interior design is when you can move around a space with unbroken continuity. It doesn't take a rocket scientist to work out that if you are stubbing your toe on a table or chair every time you go to get something from the refrigerator, it's not going to end well for your toe, or for the piece of furniture that is causing the pain. And let's talk about that door or drawer that moves like it's trapped in sinking sand rather than gliding like an Olympic ice skater. I know you've experienced this. For me, a drawer that is horrendous to open or close just ends up never being opened, so whatever I have stored in there has been lost forever. Or who has tripped over shoes in a hallway when it's dark? The natural flow has been broken by too much stuff or things simply being in the wrong place.

The better we can move around within a space without interruption, the more engrossed we become with the environment we are in, the more enjoyment we can have and the happier we can be.

I am currently facing a flow nightmare at home. I keep my bike in my little courtyard that I share with my neighbour. We store our garbage bins in the laneway to the gate that gives us access to the street. To get my bike out to ride it, I have to either move four bins every time, or manoeuvre my bike through my house. It's easy to guess how often I take my bike out.

A window linking to the outdoors is a clever way to draw a person to another level of a building.

The famous line, 'Good design is when you don't know it's designed' applies to incorporating flow into a space. Flow isn't just about creating a walking path through the house without having to trip over furniture, it also means doors opening smoothly or being able to reach for a saucepan from a cupboard with ease. Think of the beautifully designed iPhone and how intuitive the operating system is. You can move around the phone without instructions, without confusion, as it works the way our minds work. We should take this approach when we are designing our buildings and homes.

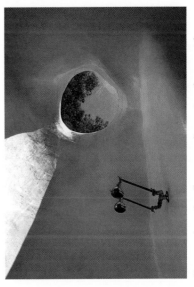

Organic-shaped walls surrounding a tiny shower with a circular skylight make an enticing space.

I have always felt that the Japanese are the masters of scale. Designers often say they nail it on the detail, but I have found the finishing on a lot of their projects raw and unpolished. Their great skill is that they understand the power of a space and the importance of creating harmony in the areas of negative and positive space.

Whether the building has a large or tiny footprint, the Japanese create areas that feel bigger than they are. Not only is a traditional Japanese home sparsely decorated with furniture and accessories, the spaces are flexible. Instead of using doors that slam shut, the Japanese use external and internal walls called *shoji*, which translates as 'interceptors'. Made from timber and rice paper, these walls are translucent, lightweight and never interrupt you getting from A to B. Buildings have partitioned walls that can be slid aside when appropriate. With an entire portion of wall removed, the room flows into a larger space or out into the garden, unifying the inside and outside. To continue this flow, the Japanese extend the timber floor from inside to outside, forming a verandah. At times this verandah can stretch past the eaves of the house to form a jetty.

A dramatic sculptural staircase found in this Melbourne home, designed by Leeton Pointon Architects and Susi Leeton, is crafted to soften the vast space.

Leeton Pointon Architects have designed a curved tiled wall to help provide more space in what would be a narrow galley kitchen. Using curtains to conceal stores gives easy access.

FLOW
Agenda

Flow

Traffic flow

Happy curves

Ever-changing space

A tall swivel door is not only visually pleasing, but saves valuable wall space in smaller houses.

Traffic flow

Ideally, all the living areas should blend into each other, creating a better
traffic flow and inviting you to use them. The only rooms in the house that
should be cut off are the bedrooms and the bathroom.

You can have minimal furniture and objects in a space but still lack flow. Homes with better traffic-flow patterns sell faster than those with dead areas, such as rooms that don't segue into other areas. I have visited so many homes over the years with flow problems. When you have rooms that are cut off from others, that don't invite traffic in, they end up being used less.

The biggest challenge is when people add an extension to an existing building. It's common to see a lack of connection to one another in either mood or feel. This absence of know-how in relating old with new can be jarring and confusing.

Other ways to achieve flow are by eliminating corridor space, knocking down dividing walls, arranging rooms so that there are internal views and vistas across a space, or even making sure a natural breeze is able to move through the house in a continuous stream.

Not only do you want to create traffic flow through the house, but you also want to make it easy to move around a room. There is nothing worse than when you share a bed and one side of it is pushed against the wall. The person who sleeps against the wall has to climb over to get in or out, and it's definitely not great if you have to get up in the middle of the night to go to the bathroom. Similarly, in the living room you always need to have space between the sofa and coffee table. If you have to stumble over furniture, it isn't pleasant. If these problems sound familiar, you clearly have your layout wrong, you have too many pieces of furniture or they are too big.

Doors, windows and staircases all play a vital role in good flow. Don't underestimate how these functional things can give you pure pleasure when moving around your home. In fact, if you've ever forgotten your purpose when walking from one room to another, don't worry. Research says that walking through doorways resets emotions and causes us to forget things. I find this an incredibly romantic concept and it fits perfectly with what we've been saying for years – when you walk through your front door, you can leave the world behind. Now there is science to back it up! This is all the more reason to put effort into your entrance to make it as welcoming and inviting as possible. However, if you are wanting to achieve flow, don't use too many doors, as things could get frustrating.

Happy curves

Many people consider curves to be a more natural environment for humans
to thrive in. Curves transform buildings to make them soft, feminine spaces.
Fluidity of a space with no sharp angles can be powerful in a building.

So much of our human-made world is made up of straight lines. There is a reason for that. Straight lines are logical. They fit together well and are easy to adapt and therefore more economical for building. Curves bring a whole other dynamic. A sweeping bend or a gentle arch can take you on a journey and create a sense of mystery. When every surface inside and out is designed to be smooth and curved, it gives a sense of uninterrupted continuity and there is a complete lack of sharpness or harshness. Rounded organic shapes and neutral colours blend in perfectly, adding to a wonderful atmosphere.

A metal spiral staircase can be somewhat questionable in a building of beauty. But a swooping staircase – like the one found in the Melbourne home designed by Leeton Pointon Architects – is a moment of awe. It's poetic, peaceful and perfect. The focal point and central pivot of the house is this sculptural, circular staircase. There is no thinking, 'Oh, I have to climb the stairs', you just do it.

Studies have shown that people tend to prefer curved objects to those that are rectilinear, whether it be tables, sofas, watches or typography. Research led by psychologist Oshin Vartanian studied people's brains while they looked at various images of architectural design. The participants were asked whether they found each design 'beautiful' or 'not beautiful'. Far more people preferred designs featuring curves rather than those with straight lines. Personally, my favourite iPhone is still the first generation 3G, with its curved edges. It may have been flawed, with cracks appearing on the curved casing, but I was devastated to hand it in for the newer, hard-edged, sharp-cornered version.

Curves appeal to the eye and the heart. This means that if they can touch our positive feelings, then they can make us feel happier. But why do we prefer them? Studies have shown that objects made with harsh lines or sharp corners affect a part of the brain involved in processing fear. Sharp objects are associated with danger, while soft curves are processed as harmless. There is something comforting about this research, but there are, of course, times when streamlined design is spectacular and circles and curves feel out of place. Just because we may have a natural affinity with curves, doesn't mean we always think they are superior. I mean, let's talk about those pyramids in Egypt...

The only problem when working with curves is that they are more difficult to get right, and this may be the reason why we see fewer buildings with sensual swoops. For example, in 2012 in Britain, the government actually banned the use of curves and folding walls when building schools, in order to cut development costs. The Royal Institute of British Architects was concerned and believed this harsh ruling would impact on the behaviour and wellbeing of both the students and teachers.

'Human beings have confined themselves to dead ends and angles that impede their movement.'
— Antti Lovag, architect

Ever-changing space

Every day is a new beginning and, with that new beginning, we need a
space to fit our needs. Happy design is flexible design. A space should be as
changeable as the moods you feel.

Some days you want to be social and have a lot of space around
you, but other days you prefer to hide in your cave – so
you need to design possibilities into your space. When I think
of sustainable homes and cities, my first thought always goes
to this quote by sociologist Leon C. Megginson, 'It is not the
strongest that survives; but the species that survives is the one
that is able best to adapt and adjust to change'.

In September 2012 it was reported that in Australia,
a new home was completed every 15 minutes in an area of urban
growth. What worries me with these quick builds is the lack of
long-term thought for the residents' wellbeing and happiness.
My dream is to work alongside a developer right from the
start, before the design process even begins, to make sure that
happiness for residents is the first priority, rather than profits
and quick sales.

The reality is that if you feed into people's desire for
happiness, you are still going to have quick sales and profitability,
but the added benefit is that developers will know they are
creating a place that people will enjoy for generations – rather
than a mere decade, if they're lucky.

Developers try to match current trends and buyers'
needs with a one-size-fits-all attitude, but this is a trap we see
too often. Within five to ten years, these properties become
highly undesirable because they have dated, the facilities don't
match new buyers' needs and often the buildings that were
made cheaply begin to look vulnerable. We need flexibility
in new developments and new suburbs.

Every well-designed building ideally has virtue,
flexibility, adaptability and endurance. In my last book,
Rethink: The Way You Live, I called this form of design 'ever-
changing space'. With housing across cities becoming denser,
we are taking guidance from Japanese homes, which are
famous for their flexibility of space. We need spaces that don't
frustrate us but are capable of bending. We cope so much
better when a room, a building – or even a community – is
malleable and mouldable. There is nothing more frustrating
when a space or person dictates how we must live. Our nature
is to rebel. Individuality will always win.

When someone tells you what your home should look
like, ask yourself, 'Who is this person? Are they happy? Do
they know me? Do they know what makes me happy?' It's like
going into a clothes shop and finding only size 8 is available.
Imagine the uproar! Designing homes with a one-size-fits-all
approach is almost the same scenario, but a much more costly
one. The less material an architect uses in a space and the less
they dictate the function of each room, the more able the
owners will be to adapt the space to their needs. Today, with
so many of us working from home, we need our spaces to be
flexible enough to work and live in. We don't know what our
life will bring, so we need a space that can flex with whatever
that may be. When your home has many possibilities, it gives
you a sense of freedom. There is no limitation when there are
no barriers between one room and the next, or from outside to
inside. It gives you a chance to look at the world differently.

VOICES

NANCY RENZI, INTERIOR DESIGNER
Sydney, Australia

'This has been the most nurturing home I have ever lived in. It's like living in a womb. I feel so safe and secure in this home with walls hugging around me. The way the building sits into the hill makes me feel calm. I don't feel like we are disturbing nature or people in this home; it just feels like it belongs here.

'In my old open-plan, straight-lined beachfront apartment the boys would hide in their bedrooms with their friends or be online. In this house the bedrooms have been designed to be small so the curvaceous home encourages us to be connected in the communal area. In the old open-plan house the television would be on all the time, but in this space it's rarely turned on. The space has really changed the way we live. The boys' friends love to hang out here and, when we are here alone, we sit in the 'conversation pit' and play music. It's really intimate there, and there is no easy way out. You need to feel good with the people you are there with. I don't invite people in there that I don't know well – it's only for family and very close friends. When the fire is on it heightens the feeling of intimacy.

'The space feels so generous but the footprint of the house isn't that big. The curves don't interrupt the place where one room ends and a new room begins.'

BUILDING HIGHLIGHT

An incredible 1971 sculptural, curvaceous home, which is nestled into a hillside, looking out onto the beautiful northern Sydney beaches.

BELIEF

Humans perform and behave better in, as well as enjoy, a curved space more than one built with straight lines.

LESSON

It's important for a curvaceous home to include some elements with straight lines, as without them, the curves would be taken for granted.

'I have to put artwork with straight lines on the walls to help balance the space. Otherwise I feel the curves become too much and can actually make me feel like I lose orientation.' — Nancy Renzi

Humour

HUMOUR IS BY FAR THE MOST SIGNIFICANT ACTIVITY OF THE HUMAN BRAIN.

Edward de Bono, *Daily Mail*, 1990

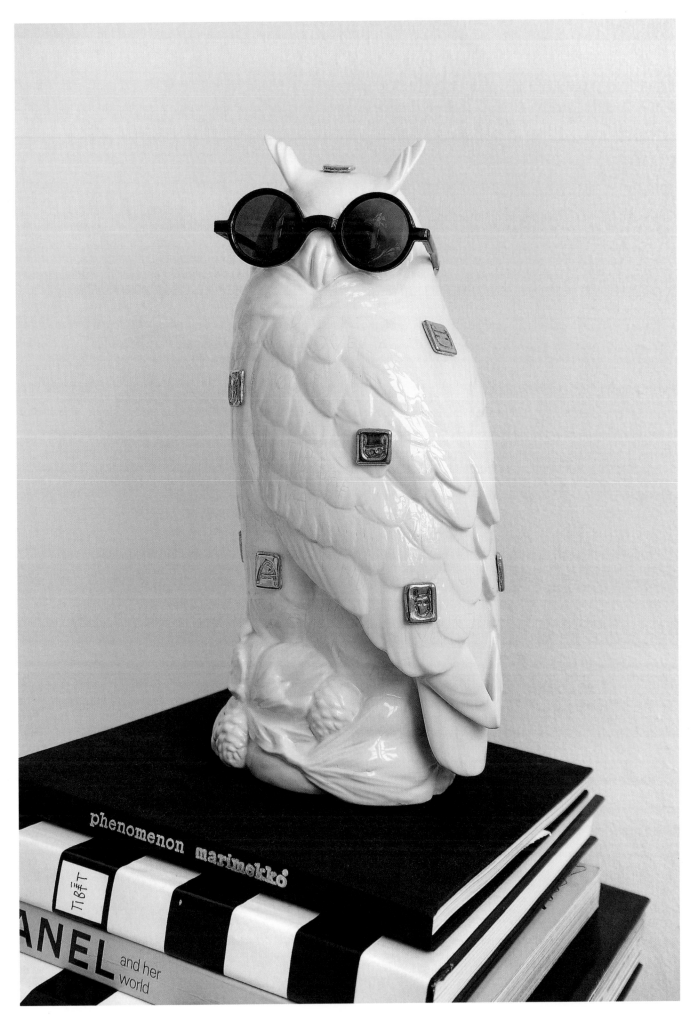

Let the laughter in

Amanda on
playful punctuations,
wit and warmth
& getting your space to crack a smile

Should we banish the whimsical and eccentric interiors that are full of humour, wit and charm to make room for only rational designs? Are you crazy? Hell, no! I believe that what is lacking in most design is humour. I would like to rectify this situation.

New York interior designer Ghislaine Viñas introduces the unexpected in what could have been a white, cold, bland room with an oversized DIY Qee Bear sculpture.

Humour

So many buildings have become anti-human by being too serious. We should be more daring and true to design by bringing in more personality and, of course, happiness.

A lot of design is a little bit sad. Design should be beautiful, glamourous and functional, but it should also communicate optimism and joy. When we design a space we want a classical foundation, but the trick is to add playful punctuations. For me, adding humour to a serious or melancholic space is like that moment in *The Wizard of Oz* where Dorothy first opens the door from the sepia tones of Kansas to see the colour of Oz for the first time. It's the eccentric, bold, colourful, witty and very personal homes that I have always loved and remembered.

It's the little added details, like this multistriped sock, that add wit to Moooi's iconic horse light, designed by Swedish design group Front.

I think many designers dislike the idea of adding wit to a space because they think it might cheapen the experience. This is madness. They need to loosen their tie, undo their top button and relax. We have to look at the funny side of things and be able to laugh at ourselves. The only consequence you face with humour is that it will make your design approachable and fun. It's the little gestures – a smiling orange animal ornament or a funny message on a wall – that make a home enjoyable and memorable.

It is our choice how serious or joyful we want our life to be. The last place in the world that should be serious is our home. I'm not suggesting you turn your home into sideshow alley (although that sounds like fun), but do integrate some lightheartedness into your serious design ideas. A building can be beautiful and high-minded while still being happy. Witty design not only makes us smile and laugh, but also demonstrates the designer's intelligence; their knowledge of how to amuse people and enliven life.

An unexpected pop of colour has been used to improve the look of an intimidating, utilitarian security camera.

Humour in design used to belong only to the brave and eccentric designers. That's why designers like Verner Panton, Jonathan Adler, Dutch designer Hella Jongerius and Spanish-born Patricia Urquiola, who all create amazing pieces and places that can't help but make us smile, have become so popular.

On the busy streets of New York, an enticing little mouse door has been installed for the resident cat Thomas.

Take inspiration from these pros and infuse your spaces with playful items. Get your space to crack a smile, add a dash of the unexpected and let your true personality emerge through your decor, using the charm of shapes, colours, materials and animals. Laughter is such a vital part of our lives, and I hope we will see more buildings and spaces in the future that will be designed to help trigger a snort, giggle or chuckle.

To add those feel-good moments to your walls, commission an illustrator to create a bespoke work of art. This illustration is by Mark Mulroney.

While I was styling his house for the book, it was a very happy moment when I pulled back the bed sheets from Jonas Bjerre-Poulsen's bed to discover this 'Nordic Elements' bear duvet.

HUMOUR
Agenda

Lighten up
Be optimistic
Friendly spaces
Be unpredictable

The aptly named 'Cloud House' by Australian firm McBride Charles Ryan is proof that an extension doesn't have to be just a glass or wooden box.

Lighten up

The design world is in need of a little lightening up. It's psychologically, and even physiologically, important to create interiors that amuse and entertain us. The simple act of a smile or laugh sends a message to your brain that you're happy. This then causes feel-good endorphins to be released, which can help reduce blood pressure and anxiety, regulate blood sugar and improve digestion. There's nothing better than that moment where we double up with helpless laughter that hurts our ribs and face. Laughing is contagious. When we hear someone laugh, we want to know what's going on, so we can join in. Actually, you are 30 times more likely to laugh if you are with somebody rather than being on your own. Laughing with others has an important social function, too, as it helps us to bond and maintain friendships.

I have visited some unhappy places in my life, and institutions for the elderly and homeless have been especially dire. No matter what your socio-economic situation, location, culture or age, everyone deserves spaces and places that encourage them to be happy. We shouldn't overlook the importance of a good old-fashioned giggle, even in healthcare institutions, but you need to understand what makes the people who live or work there tick. Remember, what you may find laugh-out-loud funny may not make your client laugh. It's their humour you need to tap into.

Be optimistic

I don't know about you, but I am ready for a break from bad news. There seems to be a constant barrage of it around me. Therefore, it's not surprising that we see so many people drowning in depression, fear and anger. If you are trapped in dark moods it's so much harder to see a logical way out, and a little problem can seem so much bigger than it actually is. When times get tough, it's important to focus on the positive.

Optimistic design demonstrates opportunity, and takes an approach where problems are solved, constraints are moved and behaviour is changed for the better. Optimistic design is a little outspoken and bright, and is sympathetic and generous. In the 1960s, British designer Sir Terence Conran created an iconic design look full of optimism with a fresh and happy colour palette, natural textiles and simple geometric forms. Today, optimistic design is again expressing hopefulness and confidence about the future. We are seeing traditional designs being revamped with cheerful colours and graphic prints.

One thing for certain is that most of us believe we are optimists. In the Happy Poll, 88 per cent of people said they were. This is fantastic news, because positive emotions help to expand vision, and to relieve anxiety and physical stress. When we focus on the positive, we not only feel happier, we flourish.

Friendly spaces

'Make your home friendly and welcoming' is perhaps an obvious statement. Friendliness and happiness go together like strawberries and cream. When setting the mood for a space, why not personify your objects, textiles and colours by simply asking which ones you want to be friends with? A good way to pick items for the home – say, for example, a tap for the kitchen sink – is to look at the different varieties on offer, their shapes and material, and see if you prefer the blobby, jovial shape; the sleek and witty shape; the loud, opinionated shape; the traditional, handsome but cheeky style; the sexy eco-warrior; or the shy but thoughtful shape. It's a fantastic way to stay in line with the happy, friendly, fun mood you are trying to achieve and it's an extremely enjoyable way to draw inspiration.

A cheerful, welcoming house gives you a spring in your step. It feels 'bright and light' and invokes a sensation that things are going your way. The materials and colours and patterns are full of charm, warmth and sincerity. A friendly space is a place to spend time with friends, enjoy special occasions, receive and give gifts or get some unexpected good news. You will generally find that friendly homes are injected with humour, too. When designing your home, make sure you include designs that your partner loves and finds amusing, as increasing your partner's happiness will improve your own.

Be unpredictable

The unexpected brings the fun into your home. By using unpredictable colours, forms or textures you can give life to a space and bring a smile to people's faces. Try masculine versus feminine features, or unusual details such as using a vintage mirror for a dining room table, wallpapering your toilet in an oversized print, using toughened glass for the floor, or finishing a ceiling with high-gloss paint. The more inquisitive you are, the better your chances of discovering something new or unexpected. And it's fun.

Good design almost feels 'revealed' rather than 'created'. It looks like it was always there waiting to be discovered. While I was travelling across the globe, researching this book, I visited a couple of places that, at first glance, seemed like really serious design spaces, where the personal expression of those who lived there was lacking. However, that was until I pulled back the covers on the bed. In one house, I found a grizzly bear printed on the duvet below the covers, and the other revealed a sparse pattern of polka dots. These were the only two homes where I didn't actually get to spend time with the owners, but when I saw those fun and unexpected prints, I immediately knew I'd love them anyway. Those little hidden gems demonstrated the owners' humour, which instantly made me feel warm and welcomed even though they were not there.

Something new or different, not usually seen in a design, draws our attention and fills us with a sense of possibility. It triggers our fascination and entices us to explore and unearth what else a space might be hiding. The unexpected stimulates the positive emotions we feel when we are learning and discovering.

Find your funny bone

Perhaps you need help in finding your funny, optimistic bone. You can use the list below to help you get going. When you answer the following questions, ask yourself what you could do to cultivate the feeling and display it in your design.

1. When was the last time I smiled or laughed out loud?
2. Where was I?
3. What was I doing?
4. What else gives me that feeling?
5. Can I think of other triggers?

Chapter Six

VOICES

PRIVATE OWNER
The Cloud House, Melbourne, Australia

'We wanted our home to be fun and a place that lends itself to good times. It's such a playful addition to have the outline of a childlike impression of a cloud. As a family we love spending time here and our friends always want to come for barbecues and parties. When we first moved in, our young son would run up and down the hallway and lie down on the floral carpet as he loved the colour and bold, fun pattern.'

BUILDING HIGHLIGHT

A traditional, Edwardian-fronted home with a very untraditional cloud-shaped extension. The warming red kitchen is literally the heart of the home and bridges the old and new architecture.

BELIEF

Designing the building you live in is a state of mind. It's hard to define happiness but, once you decide you want a home that makes you and your family happy, you are on the path to being open to new ideas.

LESSON

The more serious your work becomes, the more important it is to live a life and have a home that makes you smile, laugh and have fun with those you love.

'I often forget I live in a cloud, but those who visit for the first time get to experience a space that pays homage to the unexpected. I love seeing the expressions and how they act in our space.'

VII

Lighting

LIGHT, GOD'S ELDEST DAUGHTER, IS A PRINCIPAL BEAUTY IN A BUILDING.

Thomas Fuller, *The Holy State and the Profane State*, 1642

Light up your life

Amanda on
light and happiness,
guiding light
& clever lighting

Imagine the days of candlelight, oil lamps and gas lights bringing a dancing and flickering dim light to our domestic interiors. Families would commonly huddle around a table to read, sew, play cards or simply chat. Even today, when we have so many possibilities for lighting, when it is used correctly it is one of the most evocative, feel-good tools for interior design. For example, it's impossible not to marvel at Le Corbusier's Notre Dame du Haut chapel in Ronchamp, France, or Tadao Ando's Church of

Lighting on walls, floors and tabletops gives a space incredible ambience and provokes a great mood, rather than overhead lighting, which usually flattens an atmosphere.

the Light in Osaka, Japan. The minute you walk into these churches you're overtaken by an omnipresent experience, even if you aren't religious. The lighting design in the buildings makes you feel there is more in the world than yourself, while simultaneously making you feel safe, inspired – and that anything's possible.

When it comes to our wellbeing, lighting is vital. Humankind has always identified light as a signal of safety, warmth and comfort. Before electricity lit up our city streets, darkness signified danger and people were often reluctant to go out at night. In the pre-electrical world people used to push all their furniture up against the walls, so they didn't trip over objects when the sun went down and the rooms had little, if any, visibility. In the Georgian era, furniture in the centre of a room would have been as odd as if we put a wardrobe in the centre of a room today.

Skylights are great light sources for small spaces that suffer from a lack of natural daylight.

It's not surprising, then, that we tend to feel safer when we are in well-lit spaces. The way we light our homes, buildings and even our cities can play a massive role in the way we react to them. Lighting, like colour, has an incredible influence over directing how we eat, sleep, work, recover from illness, feel happy or sad. If we sit in the wrong lighting for too long it may even lead to clinical depression.

For me there isn't anything more beautiful than a city skyline twinkling at dusk. Each light from a home or building signals that there is life inside. I confess I like to walk around cities at twilight, peering into people's homes from the street after they have flicked on their lights.

I'm fascinated by seeing how others live and the minute I see lights on in people's homes and the streets illuminated, I don't feel so alone. I feel a connection to the strangers in the buildings. It can make some of the largest and busiest cities in the world feel just that little bit more intimate.

Don't ever underestimate the power daylight has on your happiness and the feel-good factor it brings to your home.

Lighting is one of the key elements in determining whether we feel contained and comforted in a space. It can create boundaries, which in turn can suggest intimacy. On the other hand, places with too much light can make us feel exposed and uncomfortable.

Lighting is an essential layer of interior design that brings warmth and cosiness to a space.

We tend to feel safer and more at home in pools of light – think of the eternal appeal of candlelight, which is more soothing and calming than overhead lighting. Creating a lighting scheme that invokes comfort and joy at home affects us psychologically, and therefore has a strong bearing on our happiness.

Highlighting architectural detail with coloured LED lights can add those extra 'wow' factors to a building.

When we light our bedrooms and living rooms we can create relaxing atmospheres by using table and floor lamps. Make sure the light bulbs are strong enough to illuminate the room through the fabric shades.

LIGHTING
Agenda

The importance of daylight

Light therapy

Emotional lighting

Natural versus artificial light

Designing with light

LED lighting

The faceted glass with mirror trim draws natural light into the New York SkyHouse.

The importance of daylight

Too many of us are seduced by the freedom to sleep, work, eat, drink, or travel when we want, due to 24-hour artifical light. But in reality our bodies suffer an enormous strain if we ignore our natural circadian clock.

Our 24-hour body clock, or circadian clock ('circa' – about, 'diem' – a day) takes signals from the light of the sun to regulate our alertness or sleepiness, physical strength, mood and more. The rising of the sun alerts us that we should wake up and get ready for the day, while the setting sun does the opposite and our brain begins to wind down for sleep.

When designing lighting in your home, you should aim to let in as much natural light as you can in the daytime while at night you want to keep it out. In the evening, as you are getting ready for sleep, you need two hours of dim light before bed. Also, during daylight hours you want lighting to be cooler, while in the evening you want warmer light. When lighting is cooler and more intense we feel more awake and productive; warmer lighting entices us to unwind and relax.

Individuals who are exposed to dim levels of light overnight, such as a glowing television, can develop signs of clinical depression. Therefore at night we should limit our use of electronic devices. Studies have shown that if you do need a light at night, it's better to have one that gives off a red light rather than a white light. I gave it a go and swapped all my living room white bulbs to red. At first it felt like I was in a brothel, but I found the light did soothe me and my husband. Later I introduced a pink globe in the living room and I found I enjoyed this glow more aesthetically and I could see better, but it didn't have the same positive intensity on my mood as the red.

Although we are designed to rise with the sun and rest when the sun sets, modern life has imposed an unnatural order. Light pollution is the term for this artificial brightening of the night, which interferes with our natural cycles. We need to make some big changes in the way we design buildings and interiors to help us get back into rhythm with the natural order of things. Daylight boosts our mood when it touches our skin or enters our eyes. Our mood is positively influenced by ultraviolet (UV) light as it soaks into our skin. UV light is a natural trigger of vitamin D, which is not only a bone builder but also stimulates the production of feel-good brain chemicals, such as serotonin and dopamine.

Light is measured in lux. On a cloudy day, natural light from the sun measures around 10,000 lux and, on a sunny day, it can be as high as 100,000 lux. When you compare this to ordinary room lighting, at around 50–500 lux, you can see the problem. The lack of daylight is a particular issue in large institutions, such as schools or hospitals, where people tend to be isolated from daylight.

So many of us are living our lives in dim spaces, but we can let more natural light into our lives with good design. Our buildings can liberate us from the gloom by allowing our bodies to use the happy natural pattern of light and dark to optimise our biology. By using the sun as the main light source in our buildings, it can positively affect our emotions as well as helping the environment and our economy.

Light therapy

It's clear that many of us don't have enough daylight in our homes. Around 41 per cent of people in the Happy Poll indicated they wished they had more daylight inside. If you don't receive sunlight at the correct times in sufficient quantities you can upset your body clock to such a degree that you might suffer from what is known as seasonal affective disorder, or 'SAD'. If you do, there are special, medically certified SAD lamps, which can be purchased for use indoors. These replicate daylight and can provide 10,000 lux of light, which can help to improve mood and wellbeing.

Researchers are finding medicinal and psychiatric therapies in different light conditions can alleviate – but maybe not cure – mood swings. Sometimes the daily ailments associated with our extremely busy lifestyle, such as fatigue, jet lag or insomnia, can be fixed by something as simple as better lighting. Through LED (light-emitting diode) lighting, issues like jet lag may become a thing of the past. The 'photon shower' has been designed to help long-haul travellers. The idea is that a traveller enters their flight information and the photon shower will stream light into a chamber that is customised to that person's light needs. Another innovation, the Luminarium by Stefano Pertegato, works with the 24-hour body clock. This lighting system imitates the natural cycle of the sun's movement. Over 12-hour cycles the Luminarium reproduces the colour and intensity of the sun's light, from dawn till dusk. This could help people who are suffering from light-related disorders to recalibrate their bodies.

Emotional lighting

Across the globe we are seeing how lighting systems are being invented and used to trigger positive emotional responses. They can even assist in people's relationships with their family and friends. We are moving towards seeing customised, on-demand lighting experiences being available for the home.

One of my favourite innovations in lighting is the Good Night Lamp, which can assist with our emotional connection to family or friends who live far away. The concept uses the global mobile phone network to create a synced lighting experience for all those who have a lamp. The way it works is that you have a main lamp at one location, and then you set up smaller associated lamps at the homes of people living far away, even on the other side of the world, to whom you want to feel closer. So, when you turn the main lamp on or off, it triggers your loved ones' smaller lamps to do the same thing. When they see the lights going on and off, they can imagine you getting up, going out, coming home or going to bed. It's an ambient social network and makes you feel emotionally connected.

Lee Broom's basement bedroom bounces light sources from the glass walls, mirrors and reflective tiles in his ensuite bathroom to light up the dark room.

In his Tuscan home, Italian architect Piero Lissoni has used louvres to determine how much light he wants in the main bedroom during the day.

Natural versus artificial light

When it comes to using artificial lighting, I am a firm believer that, as with anything fake, you need to show control and restraint. No matter how soothing, calming or uplifting artificial lighting might appear to be, our bodies will always know it's not the real thing.

Scientist Mirjam Münch, at the Lausanne Federal Institute of Technology in 2012, compared two groups of people, one exposed to daylight, the other to artificial light, over the course of several work days. She found that the participants who were exposed to daylight were much more alert and less stressed in the evening than those who had been in artificial light. This information rocks the current trends within the interior design scene. Moody, dark inky rooms, with table and floor lights on during the day might look cool, but they simply aren't good for your happiness levels. However, at night this environment would be absolutely fine and, in fact, beneficial. With all the scientific evidence to show that daylight is a basic human need, we should be doing everything we can to let it into our buildings and lives.

If your space is lacking daylight, then the obvious answer is to install more windows. Not only do the glass panes let sunshine indoors, they are important in connecting you with the outdoors. A review of people's reactions to indoor environments suggests that daylight is desirable, both for illuminating the space and allowing you to see what you're doing, but also for you to experience some environmental stimulation.

To be healthier and happier, get back into your normal biological clock routine. Adjust your exposure to artificial light to help your body function as much as possible on the 'time zone' that nature intended.

Designing with light

I believe we have become lazy when it comes to lighting our homes. It's normal to see one garish light bulb used to illuminate an entire room. However, others overinstall bright white downlights all over the house, which are used even during the daytime. Too often we see a one-size-fits-all approach when it comes to lighting. I was surprised that 66 per cent of people in the Happy Poll use overhead lighting in their home, compared to 34 per cent who use floor and table lights.

It's not just the overall ambience that can make or break a space or room. Often, pendant, table or floor lamps look so out of place with the rest of the design. The light you choose can add real impact and character to an interior. It's the finer details of design that make a space feel exceptional.

Don't skimp on your ideas when it comes to lighting. Use lights in a shape or detail that will make you smile every time you switch them on – a worn, tattered lampshade that evokes emotions with a connection to history, or neon text that puts a happy uplifting message on the wall. Neon lighting always brings great energy to a room. It's a way to have fun and make a happy statement about your personality. Joyful typography in cheery shapes is easy to install and makes people smile. The bolder and more fun your lighting choices, the more enjoyable a space can be. You may not feel comfortable with bold colour or unorthodox designs, but just adding a light with a touch of wit can relax what feels like a very serious space. Remember, though, that it's the little touches that make a happier interior, not things that constantly scream for attention.

LED lighting

If there is no way you can get more daylight into your home, don't worry,
technology is a marvellous thing. LED lighting design has changed the
possibilities of how we light our buildings.

LED lighting can vary in intensity over time and can also mimic the properties of natural daylight, shining brighter during the day and becoming dimmer at night. Designers and architects are experimenting with this and other lighting technologies to light up our lives, by both illuminating our environments and working to make us feel happier.

With LED lighting, a single bulb can change to millions of different hues to suit your mood and the home environment. Your LEDs can now even be operated through apps on your smartphone. As well as working like a standard light bulb, LEDs can be used to create incredible visual vistas, including floors being turned into a raging river, or the ceiling creating the illusion of an open sky. LED screens on the wall or ceiling can show images of fluffy clouds blowing across the sky, creating a pleasant environment and a sense of the spaciousness and freedom we experience outdoors.

Choose the right lighting

Asking yourself these simple questions will help you decide what lighting you need for your space:

How is the space being used? • How many people will be using the space? • How often will those people be using the space? • Do you want the space to be calming, soothing, relaxing, welcoming or productive? • Do you want the space to activate silence, intimate conversation or open discussion? • Will the space change its function and purpose throughout the day and evening?

VOICES

NICOLAS DORVAL-BORY, ARCHITECT
Paris, France

'At only 20 square metres (215 square feet), the main problem we had in our home was not lack of space but lack of light. By introducing our smart artificial lighting solutions, we have managed to create an illusion of the space being much bigger than it actually is. The apartment is designed in a simple and neutral expression, without colour or particular detail, annihilating any architectural expressiveness or narrative, to leave only the logic of composition generated by light.'

BUILDING HIGHLIGHT

Lighting, not coloured paint, is used to define zones. To retain the minimal, modern and streamlined look, no overhead or ornamental lighting is used.

BELIEF

Different types of lighting used in a space can actually change a person's perception of their environment.

LESSON

Through simple ideas you can achieve a space that people want to live in, which will bring them happiness. It's possible to change the way people feel and interact in a space with the flick of a switch.

'With lighting, I want people to feel like they are being transported to different places. When the lighting changes into different colours, I want them to feel different emotions.' — Nicolas Dorval-Bory

VIII

Location

I AM HERE; AND HERE IS NOWHERE IN PARTICULAR.

William Golding, *The Spire*, 1964

Sense of place

Amanda on
the importance of location,
money versus attitude
& changing our environment

To build is to be human. To make a mark in the landscape is as important for us as
it is to find food and water. Architecture is about place as much as it is about people.
The question is, are we happier if we build a house by the sea or in a wild landscape,
compared to setting up home slap bang in the middle of a city? Wouldn't someone
with a view of a mountain or the ability to walk straight onto a beach be happier than

Australian furniture designer Mark Tuckey drives his two daughters to and from school in his rubber dinghy in Sydney, Australia.

someone looking out onto lines of smoggy traffic? Would a person or family be happier if their home was on a large, safe suburban block of land, where they can provide a bedroom for each family member and a room to service each need, rather than living in the heart of a noisy city in a cramped apartment? Surely if you lived in a wasteland or run-down tower block your optimism, sense of purpose and happiness would gradually drain away?

Louella Tuckey looks out from her bedroom window onto the breathtaking Australian coastal views, from her water-frontage home in Sydney, Australia.

When I began writing this book, I truly believed our access to feeling good, being creative or having courage was determined by the place we happened to live in. As I researched the subject further, and looked at how design could play a part, I was forced to ask some bigger questions about happiness.

In urban cities, sometimes the best place to go and escape the noise is in public gardens, where you can look up at the sky.

For example, if someone has no money, can they be happy? Are only people with wealth able to experience joy, freedom, self-expression and all the things tied up with what makes us feel good? Do we have to live in homes with all the mod cons and breathtaking views in order to live a longer, healthier and more joyful life? Are people in sunny Australia happier than people who live in cloudy Berlin?

I quickly came to the conclusion that it was really quite arrogant to ask such questions. So many of us have experienced seeing people living in extreme poverty with contented smiles and obvious feelings of happiness. So what does this mean for those of us who live in wealthier societies? Are we putting too much focus on location when we purchase somewhere to live? It seems that whether you are happy in a location or not, often comes down to attitude.

I remember a friend saying to me, 'I hate it when people complain about bad weather, blaming it for feeling unwell or unhappy. I think they use it as an excuse because they don't want to dig deeper and really find out what is making them unhappy'. We all know sunshine makes us happier, but the one thing I have been learning on this happy journey is that we do have the power to change some things, and it's those things we should put our focus on and not the things we *can't* change.

Consider the following. There are events in our life that we cannot change at all – things like the weather or the direction the earth turns. There are things that you have some control over – government, laws, work, school. And then there is the thing you can change – your environment. Let's focus on that.

Piero Lissoni's Tuscan home has been designed with oversized glazing to take in the picture-perfect landscape surrounding the building.

A highlight of the SkyHouse, designed by architect David Hotson, is in the shower. What looks like a little cupboard to store shampoo, provides a peekaboo view of the Brooklyn Bridge.

LOCATION
Agenda

Is happiness a place?

Somewhere to call home

Location, location, location

It's all about attitude

Respect

Urban nomads

Watching the waves

Living on the land

The unexpected location

Is happiness a place?

The slogan of the Tourism Council of Bhutan is, 'Happiness is a place'. A tiny country between China and India, Bhutan is quite rare in that the happiness of the population is of great importance to the government. In fact, the government measures its success by the collective wellbeing of the nation. Back in 1972, the young Dragon King of Bhutan publicly made the comment, 'Gross National Happiness is more important than Gross National Product'. Impressive! You wouldn't find many other world leaders saying that. So what makes a place happy?

It does appear it's not a specific building or view that brings us true happiness. Social design plays a bigger part in our overall life. We are seeing more urban planners and communities trying to heal their cities and make them spaces for better living by adopting a holistic view. This takes into account physical and social needs, but also emotional, psychological and spiritual requirements.

Communities with a lot of people walking and moving around, with access to green space and a strong social network, are often the kinds of places that build physical, social, mental and emotional health and a sense of wellbeing. The future for happy cities is in how well they are working for their residents. We want cities that promote happiness by providing reasonably priced housing together with plenty of easy access to leisure and cultural amenities, efficient public transport and safe areas for children to play. The more we feel our cities are beautiful, clean and safe, the more likely we are to be happy living in them.

Somewhere to call home

No matter what our living conditions, humans have a need for a place they can call home. A sense of place is important to our sense of security, identity and belonging, and it provides us with the services and facilities needed to support and enhance our lives.

When I visited a care facility for homeless people who were recovering from illness, it was interesting to see that each resident had put pictures on the wall above their bed and personal belongings on their bedside table. The small area around each bed was decorated like a room or home. Each little space displayed the personality of the resident who lived there. These homeless people had a sense of place and quickly transformed a blank space to become identifiable as their own.

Home is a place that centres us – a place from which we set out each morning and to which we return every night. For many people, the sense of attachment to a home can become so strong that it is a part of their emotional identity. When I was young, I lived in a little country town called McLaren Vale in South Australia. I loved our home, our community and the street I lived on. When my family moved to another town in the suburbs, which had no sense of community, I was devastated, and it had a big impact on me for many years.

The top 10 happiest countries

1. Denmark
2. Norway
3. Switzerland
4. Netherlands
5. Sweden
6. Canada
7. Finland
8. Austria
9. Iceland
10. Australia

Using data from the Gallup World Poll, researchers attempted to rank countries on a 'happiness' scale. Things like life expectancy, freedom to make life choices and social support were taken into account. It was found that the world has become 'a slightly happier and more generous place over the past five years'.

'Whenever we feel slightly overwhelmed we look up,
and seeing the water instantly calms us down.'
— Mark Tuckey, furniture maker

Location, location, location

Think carefully before you make your move. We always hear that 'the three Ls' – location, location, location – are apparently what we need for the ultimate happy home. So does that mean we need to move to a tropical island to find happiness? If we don't have a vista are we doomed to be depressed with our living conditions?

Where we live and what views we have access to do seem to play a partial role in our happiness. For example, in 1986 a study took place using prison inmates who had different views from their cell windows. Those with views of mountains or fields tended to have significantly lower rates of stress-related sick calls than inmates who only had a view of the prison yard or other buildings. Also, inmates whose cells were on the ground floor – so they lacked privacy from passersby – experienced higher levels of stress than prisoners on the second floor.

It seems that natural views from windows do make a difference to our health and wellbeing. When we are surrounded by natural scenes we are happier, have more energy and feel way more relaxed.

We should consider, though, that for the prisoners – who were incarcerated, and in a poor frame of mind – their location within the prison was a vital factor. Most of us, however, can do what we want to fix up the interior of a building if the outside isn't desirable.

It's all about attitude

I believe that if we don't live in the ideal location, then it's all about attitude. Approximately 40 per cent of our happiness is directly determined by how we relate to problems, so it's not the problems that are killing us or making us ill, it's the way we deal with them. I'm not being naive. I know some places are full of violence or poverty. But scientific studies show that our life circumstances only affect 10 per cent of our happiness.

I know a couple who live in a shed at the back of a garden nursery. The vista is not pretty, there is little privacy and safety isn't great. Most people, if they found themselves in this situation, would not cope. But this couple have made the most of their home and their situation. They look for the positives, such as, 'We are saving money', 'It's really nice when the nursery closes, and we can walk around the lovely trees and visit the chickens and ducks', or 'We can paint the shed in the happiest colours'.

I previously thought it was always the surrounding landscape and location that played such a massive part in our happiness. But, if things are bad outside, then you need to focus on the inside and create an oasis that brings you comfort and joy. After seeing where my friends lived at the nursery, and observing how they created one of the happiest places I have been to, I know it's possible.

Respect

The more undesirable a location, the more design is needed to help achieve a better quality of life. I have found that when care has been put into good public design and engages us, then we seem to respect the building or street furniture more. It is less likely to be vandalised, as more of us want to enjoy it – little respect is given to an ugly mass-produced concrete bus stop.

A fantastic example of where good design has created respect in a not particularly desirable urban location, is in a building called 'HOUSE House' in Melbourne, Australia, designed by architect Andrew Maynard. To an existing Victorian building Maynard created a cedar-clad extension on the side of the house that faced directly onto a large supermarket car park. The wall is the street artist's perfect blank canvas. Maynard used black paint to create a simple stencil graphic of a house on the timber. Because the wall already had its own 'built-in' graffiti, it was hoped it would deter taggers. Tagging is usually done in black paint, so if the graphic was graffitied, it would be either invisible or easy to paint over. Amazingly, the street artists haven't touched the wall. It appears they respect the design of the building.

Urban nomads

We are a generation defined by mobility. With the world becoming 'smaller', more of us are following a career to wherever it might take us. Technology and the internet allow us to work and live pretty much anywhere. With more of us becoming 'urban nomads', it means a reduction in our attachment to a place. Another problem with people moving around is that families are separating, which means people are losing their support systems.

Home is more symbolic than real these days. Some travellers find comfort in packing some of their favourite items from home, such as knick-knacks or even their own pillow. It can help to reduce stress levels and improve sleep. Architect Anja Thede, who lives in Berlin, Germany, has built herself a 'Cargo Box'. It's a 21 square metre (230 square foot) box made from plywood. Inside it is a sofa bed, two folding tables, spaces for books, a wardrobe, drawers and a retractable flat-screen TV, and there is also space to hang artworks. What I love about this box is its mobility. Not only can it move around Anja's studio but, if she wished to change location to anywhere in the world, it would be possible to take the Cargo Box with her, so she would never lose connection with, or control of, her 'little world'.

The homeowners of HOUSE House, designed by Andrew Maynard, look out of their bedroom window onto a shopping centre car park.

Watching the waves

Although it appears our happiness isn't determined by the location we live in, there is proof that people who live closer to the coast can experience improved health.

There is nothing better than being at the beach, sitting on the sand and watching the waves roll in at sunset, or going for an invigorating early-morning swim or surf. There are many positive effects to be gained by spending time by the ocean – this is why doctors have been prescribing visits to the seaside for centuries. The sea air is filled with negative ions that assist our body to take in oxygen. Floating around in the water and bobbing on the waves can also help to relax our body and mind.

When I visited the Tuckey family, who live in the northern beaches region of Sydney, Australia, it was pretty hard not to envy their lifestyle just a little. To access the front door of their beach home you have to walk across sand, along the water's edge. The view across the sparkling blue water is spectacular. The Tuckeys have embraced their lifestyle with the location they live in and vice versa. They have chosen a place to live that suits them. I know some people wouldn't cope with the idea of walking through sand when it's raining or hailing. But for the Tuckeys it all adds to their happy home.

Living on the land

While I was researching the topic of living in the country versus living in the city, it got me thinking. Does our home represent security, while having open space around us means freedom? Are we are attached to one, but long for the other?

When I visited Italian architect Piero Lissoni's Tuscan holiday home in Italy, I thought I'd found paradise. The light, the views, the isolation and the ruggedness were almost haunting. How could this place not bring happiness? Piero felt that the land had 'bewitched him'. However, when Piero wanted to do something to the house or property, it seemed that the surrounding ancient landscape had other plans. The harsh sun, the strong winds and the wildlife all belonged in the landscape and the house was the guest. The challenge Piero faced was finding harmony between building and land.

Living on the land isn't about resting and relaxing. There are always things to do. But could this lifestyle make us happy? People who live in the country spend more time outside interacting with nature, they are always active, and those who live with nature stay connected with fresh produce too. Over the years so many of us have become disconnected from food, from craft, from utility. Humans have lost their association with the landscape and become entwined with urbanity.

The unexpected location

The 'housing cost burden' is a real problem in developed countries. Some people face living costs 30 per cent higher than their household income and many are getting into financial difficulty and losing their homes. With monthly housing costs rising, renters are also feeling the pinch.

It is forecast that, by 2025, there will be 27 'megacities' around the world, each with populations exceeding 10 million. This extreme growth is being referred to as a 'population bomb'. We will be seeing megacities in China, Indonesia, the Middle East, south Asia and northern Africa. With this population bomb facing all of us, especially those in coastal cities, we need to be aware that traditional house prices are going to become unattainable for the majority of people.

With house prices going up and the lack of land to build on, more people around the world are becoming inventive when finding a place to live. I have visited homes in some quite unconventional places, from a studio on the outskirts of Berlin that used to be a prison, to an apartment that was originally an old German supermarket. It was not only the unusual buildings that the owners had in common – each owner was equally proud of where they lived. They loved the story behind their building and how they transformed it to make it a home.

VOICES

CHRIS LAUGSCH, HOTELIER
The river Spree, Berlin, Germany

'Although the house is on the water and our front garden is the Spree, in our 60 square metres (646 square feet) we have been able to pack in an open kitchen, a large living room with a retractable double bed and sofa, a shower room, a toilet, a fireplace and a main bedroom complete with a double bed overlooking the water. Our houseboat has relaxing views of the river as well as the city, but keeps us in close proximity to the city centre. We designed the entire front of the boat with floor-to-ceiling windows giving us views of the bay. This wonderful view helps us leave the bustling city behind while we stare out to the open water. This isn't something most people who live in Berlin get to experience. The custom-made, low-to-the-ground sofas are perfect for dozing on, while watching the ducks swim by.'

BUILDING HIGHLIGHT

A modern houseboat filled with clever design features, custom-made furniture, floor-to-ceiling windows and an outdoor deck to enjoy Berlin's river Spree.

BELIEF

When you design a home well, it doesn't matter how big it is, or where it is.

LESSON

When you build a home close to nature, that should be your main design focus. Having minimalist interiors helps to not distract you from the all-important view.

'There is something very soothing about being able to look out the window and see the local ducks swim by.' — Chris Laugsch

195

— bel 28.9.13 ♥

MI

— Mia. 20-4-12

— yasmin 14/2/12

— Brad 19/10/12

— Gem my
four cuz ♥

— Olive
28/7/13

yasmin   6/37/11   — Ruby 21-2-12
                                    — Jade/4/12
Ash = 22/4/12 = Jade 14/2/12

Lucia 20/4/13

19/12

— Jade — spiv   Zoe Fried 28th A
                4/8/12

                Zoe fried 18-2-12

— 28-4-12 Tali — 28-4-12 — Lucia 21/10/12

                — Tali 18-3-12
/11   Olive spiv 20/4/12
                       19-2-12

—20/2/11 Jade

olive 1/10/11

3-11

— Jake 1/4/12

IX

Memories

LEARN
FROM YESTERDAY,
LIVE FOR TODAY,
HOPE FOR
TOMORROW.

attributed to Albert Einstein

Past, present and future

Amanda on
telling your story,
connecting to the past
& positive reminiscing

There isn't anything more wonderful than loving the life you live. For too long we have treated the home as a profit-making scheme, worrying about renovating a house to increase value or making money by buying and selling property, and not as a place where individuals and their families can grow. Your home should represent all things YOU! Life is about surrounding ourselves with the things that fascinate us, drive us and ultimately make us feel alive. The trick is not to store all these positive memories

Original rock chick Jo Wood's London home is layered with a lifetime of belongings that visually tell her incredible life story.

in drawers, photo albums or cupboards. Bring them out to visually tell your story in your home.

Making imaginative use of the resources you have available, can turn an old beige haze of ordinary into a home filled with things you love and make you happy. Get creative in the way you display objects and decorate a space. Let your home shout from the basement to the rooftop, 'I live here and this is who I am!'

In Piero Lissoni's Tuscan holiday home, he has filled the upstairs with a library of books, photographs and a small collection of his favourite hats.

Your home is an emotional refuge, a place where you have control. It's the perfect canvas on which to mark your life and say who you and your family are, where you have come from, where you have been and where you are going. We want our homes to not only look good, but also to connect us to our past and take us into the future.

Special ornaments and gifts should be out on display to remind you of the extraordinary times that have occurred in your life.

The role of home and sense of place in a person's life story is significant. As we age, our life story takes on added importance. It is no longer just a story but a resource that we can draw upon to remember our place in the world and our accomplishments.

Houses containing captivating collections of old photographs, unusual ornaments or other items, show us that there's usually a story to be told about that home and the people who live there. As it feels like we are always talking about what's new, it's nice for items in the house to reconnect us with the past.

Surrounding yourself with positive memories will definitely boost your happiness. Filling the home with wonderful mementos allows your mind to freely wander back in time whenever you see them. In this fast world we live in, being encouraged to stop and smell the roses is always a good thing.

Jo Wood's kitchen, designed by Ian Dollamore, is the perfect spot to prepare her organic meals.

The homes I have visited and the spaces I have designed that are filled with objects, furniture, artwork and other items imbued with memories, have always been the homes I have felt most comfortable in. The owners always seem so much more welcoming and open. Curiosity about them is sparked because there are little peekaboo moments of their life on display. In my opinion, their homes are the ones worthy of magazine spreads. I would rather see a much-cherished saggy couch than a high-end designer sofa that has never been used. I would much rather see a child's drawing in a frame than an expensive painting purchased only for its colour palette.

Our homes and our neighbourhoods are our 'memory machines'. They help keep alive some of the strongest resources that give our lives meaning and enhance wellbeing and happiness.

Jo Wood understands that in order to capture nostalgia in a room, every detail has to be 'you', from the light switches to the fringing on a cushion.

MEMORIES
Agenda

Spaces with personality

I find children's and teenagers' bedrooms the most fascinating. These rooms breathe the personality of the person inhabiting the space. If kids are given the freedom to do what they want to their rooms, they usually don't hold back. A child's room is their little world. It's way more than just where they cover the walls with posters, hide treasures and sleep. Even after we've left home, our childhood room can evoke strong feelings and memories. We can take design inspiration from this.

When visualising a home with personality, I think of Jo Wood's home in Camden, London. Jo was married to Ronnie Wood from the Rolling Stones for 30 years but, since her divorce, she has been living alone for the first time. It's clear that her house rocks her world. Her home is her sanctuary, and she has drawn design inspiration from her rock'n'roll past and her love of antiques – but she has given things a modern twist. For me, her home is like her autobiography, capturing her life to date as the wife of a Rolling Stone, a mother and a British style icon. You don't have to talk to her to get a good sense of her history and who she is. You only need to look around her home. Her memories and stories are told there, and not only from the photos and knick-knacks. Features like the skull wallpaper and an antiqued bathroom mirror with camouflaged skull give you an insight into Jo's personality.

What's your story?

When incorporating a positive autobiographical element in your design, combine evocative objects, photos, paintings, furniture, textiles, prints, colours, smells or music. I suggest you think of the most wonderful experiences of your life, relive the memories the best you can in your mind and then write down ways you can incorporate those recollections and feelings in your home's design.

Filling your home with mementos from distant travels, such as shells from a romantic stroll along the beach, or trophies that your grandfather won when he was a boy, are constant reminders of good times and who you are. Within your private walls you are creating your family's culture and traditions – the pillars of your identity.

Remember, though, when you're designing a home where several people or a family live, it's not a 'me' project. When selecting memories to incorporate into your design to tell your story, you should think about everyone who will be living in and using the space. It's a collective story.

Bring experiences home

Good experiences form powerful and meaningful memories. Research has shown that they make people happier than material possessions – they are more meaningful because they become part of your story and identity and have a bearing on your social relationships. The joy of buying a new material item is fleeting, and the initial happiness felt from buying a new lounge suite will diminish as you get used to it. Psychologists say we normally get used to a new purchase in six to eight weeks, with the initial pleasure we felt at purchase generally fading in a matter of months. The memory of happy experiences, however, and the ability for them to boost your mood, lasts far longer.

So what does this mean for our homes? Should we stop buying things for inside so we can live outside? To some extent, yes. If you have some spare cash, stop going to the shops or browsing online. Treat yourself with an experience, such as a concert, a football game or a helicopter ride, rather than a meaningless material object. Try to capture these moments – collect mementos, pick up beautiful feathers lying on the ground, buy new drinking glasses while on holiday in an exotic location. Bring these experiences back into your home.

A place to build new memories

You don't want a building to be only a 'memory bank'. You also want it to create new memories for those living there. We need to design spaces that tap into experiences and human relationships.

Too often we design a home or building based only on the aesthetics of bedrooms, bathrooms, kitchen and so on. How much more powerful would a design be if you focused on the experiences you want in your space! Being with others makes us happy; it is a basic human need. When designing we need to look at the opportunity to share life with others in a space. Jo Wood designed her kitchen and garden to be used, not just by herself and her family – she also regularly opens a pop-up restaurant there called Mrs Paisley's Lashings, which celebrates sustainable living and eating and uses locally produced or grown food. She is creating experiences for herself and also for others.

Our life events are not created only through our own actions. We need our councils and governments to invest in providing positive experiences for cities and neighbourhoods in order to have a happier population. When on my global travels researching the book, I asked people about what they thought would make a happier population in a city, their responses included: more parks and green spaces, bike trails, more hiking trails, free community entertainment and more dog-friendly beaches.

Jo Wood's home is rock'n'roll meets Marie Antoinette in style, and includes details like a skull in an antiqued mirror and a chrome clawfoot bathtub.

Savour the ordinary

When we design a space, we must not forget the areas where we experience
the ordinary, day-to-day activities. With creative design you have the ability
to turn a functional event into a more enjoyable experience.

It's about focusing on the details. Hardware on the doors and cupboards could be in colour; or the feel of a material or quality of a shape might connect it to the user. If you're designing for someone else, simply going for something you like isn't good enough. What is the connection to the user? What are they going to remember about it? What does it say about who they are and who they want to be?

I've been thinking a lot lately about technology and the marvels that it brings into our homes. However, I can't help but think of the simple designs that are going by the wayside, such as the common light switch. There is something so reassuring in the sound of that simple click. We are seeing the hotelification of our homes. The flat, emotionless control screens seem, to me, to be more complicated than they need. There is a beauty in pulling a toggle on a light, and coming home and switching the lights on is a ritual. We shouldn't overlook these practical objects.

A light switch or tap can be more than just a fitting to light your bedroom or wash your hands. Like sculptures in a museum, all 3D objects can have meaning and talk to us about significant and touching things. Yes, it's time consuming and sometimes more expensive to source or buy the more interesting option, but it's worth it. You are not just filling your home with old memories, you are creating new ones.

Try this

Think of three ordinary, everyday activities, whether it's eating dinner, washing up or having a shower. As you perform those activities, think deeply about them. Then ask yourself, 'What can I do to make this more pleasurable? How can I design something to help me enjoy this more?' Don't worry, I'm not suggesting you rip your bathroom apart (unless you want to) – but just adding a lovely hand wash in your favourite fragrance is a good start.

Family cookbook

To create some happy memories, you could create a family cookbook. Ask your family to email you copies of their favourite recipes. Use a print-on-demand service to create your cookbook. After the cookbook is completed, give your family copies as gifts. When you all use the book, or even see it on the bookshelf, it will make you feel connected with your loved ones.

Inheriting the past

When we inherit an object, when we hold it in our hands and take a moment
to think about where it came from, we are given the opportunity to think
and feel deeply about our loved ones and our collective past.

Perhaps sometimes we take our ornaments and heirlooms for granted, but they are there so we can reconnect with our feelings about people we have known, or who played a part in our distant history. Something as simple as a book on a shelf can be a symbol of your heritage. The past has immense value because it explains to us who we are.

After recently losing my grandparents, it hit me how important it was to own a few of their possessions. At first when I was told to pick out some of their things, I got caught up in the big picture about our life possessions, which I discussed in the Edit chapter. When I pulled a handful of items away from the mass of stuff piled on their family room floor, the things I had chosen seemed a little odd to my onlookers – an old retro teaspoon that reminded me of holidays in their caravan, two plastic containers that they had owned since I was born (one was used to house their loaf of bread and would sit on the breakfast table – my grandfather used to eat two slices of bread every morning, with lashings of margarine and lime marmalade), an old metal container my nana kept cheese in (she use to grab it out of the fridge when she would make me a cheese and pickled cucumber and tomato sandwich), and the final thing was some doilies. I have never been a fan of doilies, but they now sit proudly under some of my favourite items at home, including a Jonathan Adler ornament he gave me when I did a photo shoot with him. Every time I see or use the items I think of my grandparents. I never particularly fancied their home decor style, but now their pieces make sense and bring meaning to my home and my life.

VOICES

JO WOOD
Camden, London, United Kingdom

'I believe there is a new type of luxury. Comfort is a kind of luxury. It's about making people feel indulged. To me, a soft bed with beautiful sheets is ultimate happiness. When I walk inside my house and shut my front door it makes me so happy. I love being home and being here on my own. I love to have books around me and flowers are important too. I simply couldn't breathe if I was put in a white, minimalist space with no art or personal belongings. It would be so cold and unemotional. This is the first home since my divorce that I have been able to decorate just for me. It has been so liberating not having to take anyone else's tastes on board. I have designed this home to tell my story and share what is important to me in my life. I think this is vital for anyone who is trying to find who they are again.'

BUILDING HIGHLIGHT

A five-bedroom Georgian house decorated with a mix of rock'n'roll chic and boho cool. The space is full of one woman's incredible memories.

BELIEF

A house has to feel homely and the only way to do that is to fill it with the things that have meaning to you.

LESSON

You can't let your home become a museum. It has to hold the past and the future, new dreams and ambitions.

'My home style is my personality. It's very Marie Antoinette meets rock'n'roll. I want it to be romantic and show off my life.' — Jo Wood

Nature

NATURE ALWAYS WEARS THE COLORS OF THE SPIRIT.

Ralph Waldo Emerson, *Nature*, 1836

Green inspiration

Amanda on
nature's positive effects,
the need for green spaces
& bringing the outside in

Nature is fuel for the soul. Just being outside makes us feel more alive. Enjoying nature results in us not only feeling calmer and happier but also more focused, disciplined, healthy, social and creative. It heightens our physical and mental energy, and exercising or working outdoors can also bring a significant boost to happiness. After all, our best ideas often come not when we are in the office, but when we are outside taking a walk, sailing a boat on the water or playing with a frisbee in the park.

In the centre of a Copenhagen park, MLRP architects transformed an existing graffiti-plagued playground building into an inviting and reflective structure.

Nature

It's been shown that nature can improve our health. When feeling really sluggish, stepping outside your home or building and being in nature is an infinitely better way to get energised than reaching for a cup of coffee. The more time we spend in a natural environment, the more likely our immune system will be boosted. Even just looking at views of nature can reduce stress, and having windows with a natural vista in hospitals can help people recover more quickly. It's been found that looking at nature activates the parts of the brain that are associated with optimism and emotional stability.

Families play and interact in front of the funhouse mirrors in this Copenhagen playground.

Spending time in nature not only makes us feel better, it can actually cause us to behave better. We tend to be more caring and generous when we commune with nature. Research from the University of Rochester in New York shows that when we are exposed to nature, as opposed to human-made environments, we are encouraged to get in touch with our basic values, leading us to better appreciate both our close relationships and our community – and we are also more generous with money. Nature affects our overall life satisfaction about a third as much as getting married and a tenth as much as having a job.

With 70 per cent of the world's 10 billion people living in cities by 2100, our future wellbeing and happiness are at risk, so creating green spaces in cities needs to be a priority for urban planners and architects. Integrating nature into urban environments, including parks, vertical and rooftop gardens and so on, will help build a stronger sense of community among residents.

Researchers from the University of Illinois found that after interviewing residents of a housing development in Chicago, mental fatigue was lower in greener areas, as were rates of aggression and violence.

The mirrored gables create a sympathetic transition between the human-built and the landscape, and reflect the surrounding park, playground and activity.

Connecting the outdoors to the inside isn't a new concept. Architects like Frank Lloyd Wright, Ludwig Mies van der Rohe and Peter Zumthor have all been great masters in understanding the importance of humans and nature coming together in the living environment.

The rooftop of a weatherboard home is camouflaged with grass.

It is no longer just in homes and buildings in warmer climates where we are seeing architects pushing the boundaries of what is inside and what is outside. It has become increasingly important, and more common for buildings all around the world, to block out an uninspiring urban view with natural elements. Designers should continue to strive to work the landscape and the building together to become one.

Interior designer Nancy Renzi built an outside fireplace for her entertaining area so she could enjoy the outdoors all year round.

Architects Augustin und Frank help city folk surrounded by concrete to connect with nature by creating little moments framing plantlife and blocking out all things human-made.

NATURE
Agenda

227

For the future wellbeing of our planet, we need to stop cutting down trees in our cities and integrate more greenery around, in and on our buildings.

The importance of trees

A tree-lined street is not only beautiful, it has a significant effect on our happiness. A study in the United Kingdom followed 10,000 people from 1991 to 2008, as they moved around the country. The findings showed that no matter how much the people earned, whether they were in a relationship or not, how healthy they were, or how nice their home was, the greener the neighbourhood the happier they were.

Trees are vital to our cities. They provide shade, but they also act like natural air conditioners. Plants cool themselves and the surrounding air, and areas with plenty of vegetation release water, which helps to reduce heat. Cities can be five to ten degrees hotter than the surrounding suburbs due to a lack of greenery. With the rapid growth in urban development and, as a result, the removal of trees, considerable pressure is put on the few trees that remain in cities.

Of course it's financially more attractive for property developers to remove trees. Less trees frees up space for more buildings to sell. The scarcity of plants in the urban landscape is causing a new-world problem known as the 'heat island' effect. Heat islands are caused by the heat absorbed and radiated by the masses of concrete and bitumen (asphalt) in our cities. As cities grow, so does the number of concrete buildings and bitumen roads, and further heat is released by trucks, cars, trains, streetlights and electrical appliances. Emissions of greenhouse gases all contribute to trapping more heat and can significantly change the climate in our urban areas.

The solution is to cover surfaces with plants, which are always cooler than stone, bitumen or concrete. More large parks, vertical gardens, gardens on rooftops and balconies, trees in backyards, vegetation on streets and turf on footpaths will all help with urban heat. In the long term, creating urban forests will be good, not only for the environment, but for the overall happiness of the citizens.

Barefoot in the grass

Walking barefoot always feels good. Just wiggling your toes in the sand at the beach or running barefoot across the grass in the park for half an hour a day can improve your wellbeing and have a positive physiological effect on your body. However, when we wear shoes, this prevents us from connecting with the earth. There are communities around the world, including the Society for Barefoot Living, who walk barefoot everywhere. These 'earthing' enthusiasts believe they experience noticeable effects of grounding when barefoot, including feeling calmer, more peaceful and less stressed, and they also notice they sleep better. It also apparently assists with digestion, immunity levels, muscle tension and even hormone regulation.

In design we often say how important it is to stimulate the sense of touch. Walking barefoot in a home with natural stone or timber flooring, or woollen carpet, has an incredibly soothing effect. When we use synthetic materials, we are robbing ourselves of the natural power of the earth and its products to make us feel good.

There has been an alarming rise in the use of artificial lawn due to its low-maintenance properties. Natural turf is being replaced with synthetics for stadiums and sports grounds and even domestic lawns. Some varieties of artificial lawn look very much like the real thing and sometimes better. But the rubber underside of the material is made from old tyres that may contain harmful chemicals. Almost 10 years ago synthetic turf was actually banned in Norway and Sweden and, in Australia, a group of doctors and scientists is calling for a halt to new synthetic-turf fields. Artificial lawn is damaging to the environment but, aside from this, the artificial grass works like a pair of shoes, preventing us from having direct physical body contact with the earth. This is sad, as it seems that being barefoot on a natural surface can actually help you live a happier, healthier life.

A happy planet

Nature reminds us that we are part of something bigger than ourselves. This is why it's so important that our cities prioritise green spaces, so we always have nature at the forefront of our mind. Now is the perfect time to express that, by building a community that helps sustain our natural environment. A happy planet means a happy us.

However, there seems to be an unstoppable urban boom. The question so many are now asking is not how to curb growth, but how to make our cities sustainable. We know that urbanisation is escalating global warming. And the US National Center for Atmospheric Research says that the influx of rural populations into cities, especially in developing countries, could raise greenhouse gas emissions by a further 25 per cent by the middle of this century.

It all sounds doom and gloom, but we need to be aware of our surroundings. We should know that our planet is crying out for our help. When we understand what's happening to our earth, just like a farmer who loves their land, we can strive together to make a difference.

The more nature is pushed further out from sprawling suburbia, the more we need to connect to our natural environment. If you live on the eighth floor of a high-rise block, you can be totally unaware of what's going on outside. I used to live on the eighth floor – so many times I used to go down to the ground floor to discover it was pouring with rain, and had to go back up to the eighth floor to get my umbrella. We need architects to take into account our buildings' connection to light, shadow and wind. Somehow these fundamental elements have often been forgotten during our huge building boom.

Green housing

A 'green' housing boom is under way. There is an increase in demand from buyers and renovators in the housing market wanting properties to be energy-efficient and preferring sustainable materials. According to the National Association of Home Builders in the United States, 'green homes' will have grown from 17 per cent of the residential construction market in 2011 to 38 per cent by 2016, with a five-fold increase in revenue.

The good news is that future architecture may be more responsive to weather fluctuations. 'Protocell cladding' uses bioluminescent bacteria on building facades to collect water and sunlight, thereby helping to cool the interior of the building as well as produce biofuels. With more of them including vertical gardens, our vertical buildings will thankfully turn into 'breathing machines'. Mixed-use buildings in urban development will rely on vertical gardens that will serve as a 'lung'.

Copenhagen has consolidated its position as the ecocapital of Europe in recent years, the culmination of policies that go back to the 1970s. Copenhagen city planning gets people out of their cars and encourages them to walk, by having the the world's largest pedestrianised street in Strøget. In addition, the average Copenhagen citizen spends an hour of every day on the beach or at a sea swimming pool. With 60 per cent of local residents able to walk to natural areas within 15 minutes, this is not only aesthetically good, but of great benefit to the population's health and happiness.

'Only spread a fern frond over a man's head and worldly cares are cast out.' — John Muir, naturalist

From paddock to plate

As the world's population grows, food production becomes an increasing concern and there is a greater focus on transparency. We want to know where our food comes from so we can make more informed choices about what we eat. With our food sources possibly being genetically modified (GM), or treated with harmful chemicals without us knowing, we should worry about the harm this could be doing to our bodies. Too many of us seem to be forgetting we haven't always lived in these urban conditions. It's only in the last two hundred years that we have lived in an industrial and technological age.

The age of the celebrity chef has opened up our eyes to the wonder of good food, with an ever-increasing selection of new experiences to enjoy, often with a focus on fresh, local and sustainable product. We are starting to see restaurants, businesses and households hiring gardeners to tend their edible gardens. It makes us feel more confident in knowing where our food comes from. We are also seeing restaurants and chefs proudly displaying the provenance of their ingredients on the menu.

Imagine a time when shopping for your fresh produce becomes a thing of the past, because virtually everything you need can be grown in your own garden. People, such as designer Werner Aisslinger in Berlin, are showing exciting examples of how the kitchen garden can become a mini farm. He has designed a kitchen where mushrooms are grown using coffee grounds, with an aquaponic fish farm, where the fish waste is used to fertilise vegetables.

The future kitchen

We all know homegrown produce tastes better than store-bought. If you are lucky enough to have the space, you can create your own edible kitchen garden. You are less likely to waste your food if you have spent months tending to your garden – it won't moulder in the refrigerator like supermarket vegetables. And being productive and working outdoors with your hands in the earth always feels so good. Soil on your skin has actually been shown to boost the feel-good chemical serotonin in your brain.

Many city folk live in cramped apartments or high-density housing, and are lucky to even have a balcony. Designers looking for new and clever ways to make the most of small spaces are turning to microagriculture.

Just for a moment imagine the dream kitchen of the future. Visualise picking fresh vegetables and herbs from your own home farm. Even if you had a small space, you could keep quails to provide fresh eggs, or maybe you could have an aquaponic garden and farm your own trout! Many early adopters, who are lucky enough to install a kitchen farm, will substitute their gardener with a personal farm hand who will visit once a week to take care of crops and livestock. New technologies will help. Cold larders and recycling facilities will be seamlessly incorporated into kitchens to help keep food cool. LED lamps will be used to help cultivate produce, and self-maintaining biospheres will be set into walls for the time-poor gardener.

Horticulturist Daniel Bell has planted a variety of species on this London pub, which provide verdant growth all year round.

Use natural materials

We would like to get away from our concrete jungles, but it's often not possible. Therefore we need to find ways of connecting with nature when we are indoors. We can do this by surrounding ourselves with plants, organic objects and even images of the natural world, from tropical beaches to lush green forests. When designing, use solid, robust timbers, stone and metals that are found in the great outdoors. A slab of wood, a chunky woollen knit, crisp breathable linens, aging leather, an indoor garden or natural wall treatments are all fantastic ways to bring nature into your home. Let the objects remain weathered and use earthy muted colours that are found in the ocean and the landscapes close to your home. Wallpaper or artwork featuring landscapes look spectacular, but can also bring a calming presence into a building.

Happy houseplants

A potted plant will improve your mood. If you don't have a houseplant, today is the day to go out and purchase one. Plants also make the perfect gift for a friend.

Make sure you put your happy plant in the area of your home you use most. And don't limit yourself to one or two. The more plants you have, the more they will improve your mood and benefit your health. Plants help reduce harmful toxins in your home. About 91 per cent of people in the Happy Poll said they had fewer than 10 plants in their home. We are clearly not aware of the importance of our indoor green friends.

Most houseplants prefer plenty of light, but don't worry if your home doesn't fit the bill. There's a suitable plant for every household, from the low-maintainence *Dracaena* genus that tolerates lower light levels – I love the lush citrus shades of the 'Lemon-Lime' variety – to humidity-loving ferns, which are ideal for bathrooms.

235

Chapter Ten

VOICES

MICHAEL LEETON, ARCHITECT
Melbourne, Australia

'Bringing the outside in has become an overused phrase recently. I think it's more about connecting disparate things at the one time – a sort of chance meeting. One of the ways this connection between outside and inside can occur is framing a view and making the space or object you are looking out onto something special. It's about elevating its qualities so that we understand and appreciate it more.'

BUILDING HIGHLIGHT

A two-storey home on a steep site with understated, gently sloping, roughly rendered walls and a curved concrete roof connecting with the landscape.

BELIEF

When human-built form and nature coexist, where they share the same space and work in tandem, this can create a great tension and energy.

LESSON

Bringing two seemingly unconnected things together highlights their individual qualities and allows us to look at them in a different light.

'We don't distinguish between interior, built form and nature, they're all an extension of the same thing and their particular qualities are heightened by their proximity to one another.' — Michael Leeton

XI

Order

SPACE AND LIGHT AND ORDER. THOSE ARE THE THINGS THAT MEN NEED JUST AS MUCH AS THEY NEED BREAD OR A PLACE TO SLEEP.

Le Corbusier, architect

Get organised

Amanda on
purpose and direction,
getting control
& being more productive

Making lists, having control and living by rules all sound like things that make us unhappy and, yes, to some extent they are when we take them to extremes. But every home, building, person and society has to have a framework within which to live, in order to prevent total disorder. The fact is, humans don't do well in chaos. When life feels out of control we generally lack concentration, find it hard to relax and become

Tying together the concept of display with the spectacle of everyday life, this three-storey Japanese house and shop, divided by a single wall of shelves, has been created by ON design.

agitated. We need purpose and direction to be happy. When there is order, it gives us a greater sense of security and safety.

Teach your children early that everything has a place. Have good storage where they can put their toys.

The *Oxford English Dictionary* says, to have order in our home is an arrangement of things in relation to each other according to a particular sequence or pattern. When we have control over the stuff in our home it gives us a sense that we have control over the rest of our life.

Order in my life and home is my Achilles heel, and I can tell you that it most definitely affects my ability to be as productive as I'd like. After all, it's not easy to conquer the world, tame the universe, and be all that you can be when you're surrounded by clutter and chaos!

When we have order in our life it gives us a sense of control, which helps us to take time to savour moments.

The word 'order' actually makes me unhappy. The very thought of coming up with storage solutions makes me anxious. I was particularly worried about writing this chapter and, sure enough, I procrastinated and kept

leaving it until last. This is because I know that order and organisation are the things I need to do the most work on. But, as with anything I'm not good at, I make it my challenge to become the best I can be.

A great idea to help with order in children's rooms is to have a sliding door that you can close to hide the clutter.

Being disorganised creates extra stress that you don't need. It's so much harder to concentrate, and it's more likely that your day won't run smoothly. I find it exhausting when I'm not organised – forgetting things, misplacing things or in constant overdrive because I'm running late. When our minds are distracted by these things it's nearly impossible to find our creative flow, solve problems and get things done, and even the smallest task can seem a challenge of titanic proportions.

Those of us who lack order at home usually have tunnel vision about what's possible and shut out new ideas that could solve our dilemmas. We might be fearful about the potential costs, effort and what ifs. Just as I do, no doubt you have constantly talked about fixing problems but are slow to action the changes. And when you're finally ready to make the change, it's easy to quit when any obstacles come up.

If, like me, your organisation skills are lacking, it might be time to remedy the situation and enforce a little order in your life. You may never become the poster child for neat and tidy, but even the smallest step can make a difference, and you'll be amazed how much you can accomplish when it doesn't take you hours just to find a matching pair of socks before you can start your day.

Leeton Pointon Architects installed a streamlined wall of cupboards for clothes and linens that blends into the space.

When designing, always think how a space will be used. Where will the plates and glasses go when washing up? Where can you store glass jars? Where can you store knives and forks?

ORDER
Agenda

'Containing a large open space can be achieved
by using a cargo container for a private seating area.'
— Anja Thede, architect

Decisions or habits?

Everything you do, from switching the kettle on in the morning, choosing when and how you brush your teeth, to finding a place for your keys, seems like a conscious decision, but in fact it's a habit. According to research carried out at Duke University in North Carolina in 2006, it was found that more than 40 per cent of people's actions each day were habits rather than decisions. Researcher Charles Duhigg proposes that the meals we eat, what we say to our kids at night, whether we save or spend money, how often we exercise and how we organise our home and work routines make a huge difference to not only our productivity and finances, but our health and happiness.

Wow! What if our messy home, with those scary drawers and cupboards fit to burst, is simply due to habit? But don't worry, you do have the control to change things. It might be as simple as organising one lot of shelves, or you might have to overhaul your whole house, but you need to get some order back into your life. It's practically impossible to go cold turkey and stop a habit overnight – it's easier to replace a bad habit with a better one. We simply need to create habits that work for us.

Often when I talk to people who feel they have lost control in their home, it usually comes down to the space not coping with the number of belongings. When I help to break the problem down with them, it boils down to their habit of buying too much stuff, not being able to let go and falling back into the same routines of how they store things.

Swap bad habits for good ones

Once you identify a habit that is getting in the way of bringing order into your life and home, look at how you could introduce a new, positive habit. For example, instead of just staring at the kettle in the morning while waiting for it to boil, why don't you do a little five-minute tidy?

However, change can feel isolating, and it can seem even worse if you're feeling out of sorts, so include the people you live with to help bring order into the home. It's much easier than doing it on your own.

Start looking for patterns that are causing chaos or triggering unwanted actions in different areas of the home. Then think about how the problem makes you feel and how you react to it. How did you come unstuck? Write it down to help you get some insights. When insights emerge, look at ways to change the behaviour. If everyone is dumping their stuff in the same area of the house, this identifies that you need storage in that area. Or you could fill the space with houseplants and knick-knacks to discourage people from using it as a dumping ground.

The disorganised person usually faces not only one disaster area in the home but several. When we begin to tackle the reorganising of our homes we often feel we must do it all at once. This can be overwhelming. If you overdo it, your motivation will desert you and the chance of continuing is unlikely. Treat reorganisation in the same way you've been told to approach exercise. It's better to be consistent over time rather than overdoing it in one go.

251

Help your home to help you

I can't help but think that our homes are like lovely faithful dogs. They can be a little mischievous and stubborn, but all they really want to do is please you. When you make time to train them, care for them and love them, in return you end up reaping the rewards.

Helping your home is an effective way to help yourself. Acting compassionately and doing favours for it, such as general maintenance, will improve your happiness and decrease negative feelings towards it. There is nothing worse than ignoring the dirty dishes, the cupboard door that needs fixing or the light bulb that needs changing. When you try to avoid the dirty dishes, you may go and watch some television, but the whole time you will be thinking that those dishes need doing. Before you know it, a new pile starts to accumulate and what was originally an annoying little job is now making the idea of swimming from Australia to New Zealand seem more doable.

Doing those little jobs is always worth it. Changing the sheets on the bed is a prime example of this. Waiting for your sheets to hold enough DNA to create a new human race on Mars can make it uncomfortable to sleep. Putting positive focus onto external things, such as your home, rather than internal thoughts like worries and fears, can also sometimes help alleviate anxiety.

Are you stuck in a rut?

I have always been a big believer in not always driving the same route to work or taking the same path each time you walk your dog. Mix it up. The same goes for changing your habits at home. We do the same things over and over again, and yet we wonder why things never change or improve.

It's time to shake things up. You don't have to go wild. The smallest changes can set some exciting things in motion. Try putting up a curtain with an image of a room printed on it, to cover some chaotic open storage, or get an old trophy and use it to house your toothbrushes and toothpaste on the shelf above the basin. If you normally do all of your washing on a Sunday, try splitting it up over the week so you can enjoy your weekends. If you normally have cereal for breakfast, try toast. If you consistently go to bed at nine o'clock, try staying up till ten or turn in at eight.

The good news is that a little bit of clutter isn't always a bad thing. A recent study found that mild untidiness can encourage creativity. A group of university students were split into two groups, assigned to either an orderly or a somewhat disorderly room, and they were asked to come up with new ideas for how to use ping-pong balls. The group in the disorderly room tended to be more creative. When things aren't structured people can feel inspired to shake up their thinking, but there are limits. Dirty dishes left for days generally won't help you achieve a fresh, creative mindset.

Chapter Eleven

Piero Lissoni displays his stemware in a glass cabinet, which acts as a wall divider without blocking the view of the Tuscan countryside.

Making lists

The experts say that to find order in your life you need lists. Making lists can help you gain control and keep you focused. For so many people, this task comes easily. However, for me unfortunately it doesn't. You can make a list, but don't put too much pressure on yourself if you don't complete everything on it that day. If you are like me, and reprimand yourself whenever you stray from the message – whether it's the food you should be eating or the exercise you should be doing – it won't bring a feel-good factor into your life. Happiness won't come if we obsess and feel like we're failing.

Something friends have told me is that if they are feeling overwhelmed with the amount of things they have to do, they set themselves goals and then sub-goals. Some have even said that, when they are freaking out, they set strict 30-minute timeframes for each task.

Think of three to five goals to accomplish today and write them down. Once you've done this, consider what steps you need to take in order to achieve these goals. Break each goal down into smaller sub-goals. For example, if you have to clean the bathroom, break it down into smaller jobs, like washing the floor, vacuuming, cleaning the bath and sink, cleaning the mirror and so on. The smaller tasks are more approachable, and you can deal with them one by one. It will also make you feel better, as you can tick more things off your list, and see that you are achieving more and getting somewhere.

Everything in its place

I usually find when someone doesn't like a room in their home, it often comes down to the lack of storage. When possessions threaten to take over, it's not only our daily routines that suffer, but also our fundamental enjoyment of our homes. By getting organised you will be able to carry out your domestic duties with more ease and effectiveness and, at the same time, enjoy more happiness in your home.

What I have found is that clutter is not simply too much stuff, it's also stuff in the wrong place. Look around your room right now to see what shouldn't be there. I am a believer that everything should have its own place when it comes to the home. It's one thing to have a place to put things, but it's another for you and your family to put the items back into that spot once you've finished using them.

Storage solutions certainly aren't the same for everyone. However, home stores are making their storage flexible enough for you to design what *will* work for you. Customised, fitted storage can be useful in making the most of those awkward spaces like corners and alcoves. If you are not getting your head around storage, and the only thing you can cope with is a flatpack bookcase or shelving unit, then get a professional to come and sort you out. If a designer is expensive, then hire a professional organiser to get you on the right track. I can guarantee that when all your items have their own place, you will be so much happier and more at ease in your home. You will be free to think, play and be spontaneous.

Organising small spaces

The smaller your home, the more likely you are to meet the issues of storage head-on. If you have a small space, your design needs to work harder in function and form, with every millimetre counting. Having great taste helps, but the key in a challenged footprint is the discipline required to decorate sparingly. My advice is to look at boat, yacht and caravan designs. You should be including as much multipurpose design as possible to help save on floor space. A chair should be something you sit on, store things in and it may even incorporate a light. A table can be something you work on, socialise at and eat from, but it can also provide storage, house a stovetop and double as a ping-pong table. A staircase can be an excellent place for storage and you can have an office underneath.

One of my favourite examples of multipurposing is in one of the tiniest homes I visited while researching this book. Designed by ON design partners, the three-storey, 35 square metre (376 square foot) house in Tokyo is called FIKA. It's a multipurpose house comprising both a home and a shop that sells collectibles. The home and shop are in a single three-storey space, separated by an enormous shelving unit that extends to the top storey. Customers browse the items on the shelf but, along with the products for sale, the everyday objects of the home, such as a washed teacup, are also placed on the shelves. It's an artistic display, tying together the items for sale with the beauty of the regular everyday objects.

Rituals

Having rituals is a basic human instinct. It's as natural as our need for food, shelter and love. We need to have rituals in our daily life, as they invoke unity, continuity, connectivity and respect.

Whatever the scale of the project you are working on, you should always think in terms of the place and the person who is living there – who they are, how they respond to certain things, what their daily rituals are and, therefore, what their needs are. You should be digging deep for detail. You need to ask questions like, 'Which side of the bed do you sleep on?' so you know which side of the bed the door should be on. These are the things that make a space livable or not. How many of us have stayed in hotels where you go into the bathroom and there's nowhere to put your stuff, so it goes either on the floor or on a tiny shelf where it's always falling onto the floor? It's small stuff, but if you're going to do it, do it right, otherwise it becomes irritating. I think objects should be beautiful and have a poetic essence to them, but design also needs to be functional.

Think of the home as a framework for your life. I look at the life that will take place in a space, and then I try to make a frame for that life. Capture the rhythms and rituals of your particular world – everything matters, nothing is too small to care about. In fact, often the small things are those you care about more. It could be as simple as a candle you light when you enter your home, showing your gratitude to be back in the place you feel happiest.

VOICES

STEPHEN BAYLEY, DESIGN AND LIFE COMMENTATOR
Vauxhall, London, United Kingdom

'Our home is not a showpiece. It's taken us 33 years to get the house as we have it now. It's my wife Flo's amazingly good eye and, thanks to her, we have the most beautiful objects in our home that didn't cost a cent. She knows how to collect but display things in a way that has order and impact. I tend to not listen to people. I detest fashionable trends. I'm interested in what objects mean. It's my obsession. I would rather do without until I can have exactly what I want. All the things we have out we use – beautiful everyday things.'

BUILDING HIGHLIGHT

A four-storey, stucco-fronted Victorian London terrace built in 1840. It is filled with a lifetime's collection of books and beautiful and useful objects, without feeling like a home full of 'clutter'.

BELIEF

Objects have a powerful effect on our emotions. And those objects all have their own home within a home.

LESSON

We can acquire beautiful and useful things for our home, as long as we obtain them sparingly and thoughtfully.

'We just buy what we think are beautiful objects to use and look at.' — Stephen Bayley

XII

Play

IT MIGHT REASONABLY BE MAINTAINED THAT THE TRUE OBJECT OF ALL HUMAN LIFE IS PLAY.

GK Chesterton, *All Things Considered*, 1908

Not just for kids

Amanda on
activating your imagination,
getting in touch with your inner child
& making your home your playground

As the writer George Bernard Shaw said, 'We don't stop playing because we grow old, we grow old because we stop playing'. Play is one of the basics for human survival. It has a biological place for us, which will continue to help us develop, assist with memory and keep us moving. When was the last time you played? You need to shift your idea about play being only for children. Yes, home is a child's playground, but it should

Matali Crasset designed a bed and play area for her daughter to store her books as well as an area to sit and draw.

be your playground too. Try seeing your world through a child's eyes to make your home a place that stimulates creativity, imagination, play and happiness for you and your family. We live in a time of crisis, so why not design our spaces to be places to share in pleasure, spend time with others and participate in fun.

Stylist Jane Frosh is covering her home in the Blue Mountains, Australia, with polka dots.

It's a shame that we grow up worrying about those words, 'silly', 'childish' and 'immature', and this applies to decorating as well. I always get a little nervous when people use words like 'grown-up interiors'. The emphasis is clearly more on looks rather than the human needs of those who live inside the space.

French industrial designer Mark Sadler plays foosball with his son in their Milan home.

Play doesn't have to be something you enjoy only in your spare time. It needs to be integrated into your life and ideally into the design of your home. We focus too much on the home being our place to slow down and stop. It's our respite and, in downtime, we are more likely to zone out in

front of the television, rather than engage in some kind of creative, brain-stimulating play. However, we all want our home to be a cheerful diversion and distraction from the world outside, and the best way to do this is to create a space that can activate your imagination and entice you to be silly and simply play.

Play is not only fun, it's vital to our physical and mental health. It's as important as exercising, eating well and having enough sleep. It reduces stress, boosts learning and, best of all, connects us with others. Many of us see playing board games or computer games – or even reading, making things, playing an instrument or gardening – as frivolous pastimes. But play has also been found to be central to creativity.

Designer Matali Crasset sits in her favourite chair at her Paris home, while skyping an old friend.

Apart from all of these benefits, play is simply about joy and creates a state of happiness. It enriches our hearts and the soul of our communities. Play helps to keep relationships fresh and exciting. When we play together it can enhance happiness, vitality and resilience in our relationships. Play can heal resentments, disagreements and any other painful memories, and it enables us to learn to trust each other. When we trust our partner it's easier to work together on common goals, try new things and open up to intimacy.

We seem to forget that we have one precious life. It's so easy to get sucked down in a serious world of stress with a 'can't do' attitude. I'm pretty sure in our last days on earth we would want to focus on the good times, the fun times. We need to jump, skip, splash and PLAY!

When we play and act a little silly at home with our friends and family, our endorphins kick in, making us feel happier.

PLAY
Agenda

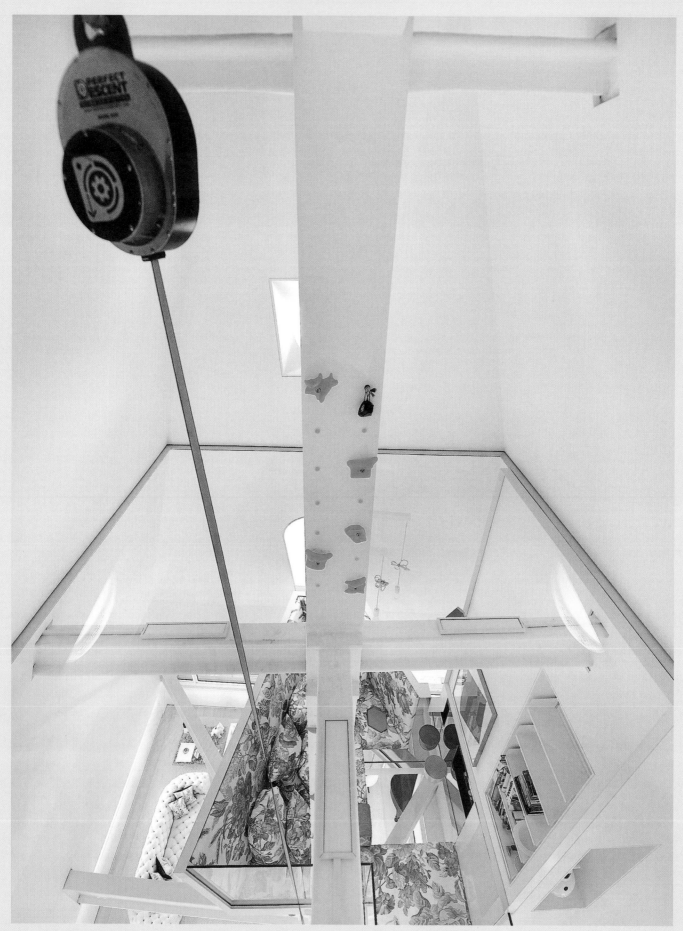

'Using minimal furniture helps activate play.'
— Ghislaine Viñas, interior designer

Play is good for our health

When we play, feel-good endorphins are released in the brain. These make us feel instantly better and happier and can take our minds off our problems or pain. Designing active play areas within your home can improve not only mental wellbeing but also physical fitness.

Older people who get regular exercise are less likely to suffer cognitive decline. Crossword puzzles, brainteasers and other thinking games seem to help too. New York architects Shusaku Arakawa and Madeline Gins, who founded the Reversible Destiny Foundation in 1987, were dedicated to creating retirement homes that reduced the ageing process. The idea was that older people shouldn't simply sit back and relax, as that would bring on a decline. Rather, they should live in an environment that stimulated their senses and invigorated their lives. Arakawa and Gins' residential homes were not designed for furniture. Among their many ideas, using natural landscapes as inspiration, seating areas were incorporated into the floor and residents had hammocks and swings to relax in.

Exercise has an overwhelming effect on our happiness and wellbeing, but we need all the encouragement we can get to do more. This then raises the serious question, 'Would we be more likely to get up and move around at home if it wasn't so damned comfortable?' Including swimming pools, basketball and tennis courts, climbing walls, trampolines or gymnasiums into buildings are all positive ways to encourage exercise but, of course, you need space. With smaller spaces and smaller budgets it's about being inventive when designing your home to stimulate movement.

Grown-up play

We know play is important for the development of our children. But we are meant to keep on playing throughout our whole lives. From the Happy Poll I found the adults with young children introduced play back into their life, but as their children grew up the activity of play exited the home. It was rare for childless individuals to play.

We ignore the young Peter Pan inside us and don't include elements in our interiors to help instigate fun and games. Take time to think like a child when you are decorating, and create enchanted spaces that stimulate your imaginations. We concentrate so much on the aesthetics of our home but just because a space is playful, it doesn't mean it needs to be ugly.

When it comes to designing play into your space, whether it be work or home, you could take a few cues from the internet giant Google's innovative offices. Known as one of the happiest places to work on the planet, much of this is due to their innovative and fun office design, which helps increase productivity and creative thinking. Instead of stairs in their New York office, they have a ladder that staff climb to reach different floors. Instead of a standard desk and chair, employees have treadmills attached to their desks. In the Zurich office they have ski gondolas, in their Dublin office there is a bar-like meeting room and in Istanbul there is a sidewalk cafe. I'm not saying you should go as big as this, but you could perhaps create what Google calls 'casual collisions', which is about bringing people together by injecting playful design ideas.

Make time for play

IKEA released the Play Report in 2010, an in-depth study about family life, child development and play. The report found that 73 per cent of children surveyed aged seven to twelve would rather play with their parents than watch television. We need to find more time for play. No matter how busy you are, always try to schedule in some unstructured time and protect your playtime dates.

We have been told for years to stop bringing out our best china (normally hidden away in some cupboard) only for special occasions, and to use it on a daily basis. I think it's time we took this approach when it comes to playing. Stop bringing out board games only at holiday times, and find ways to use them on a daily basis. Perhaps a table, wall or even a door can have a board painted on it. Could coat hooks be used so you can try to throw small rope rings onto them? Can you create secret holes through which you can pass private messages to the person in the next room? It's important to integrate breakout areas that encourage us to jump up and down or climb up a wall.

Play can be all manner of things. People in the Happy Poll shared some of their playful activities at home: dancing, playing with the dog or cat, computer games, crosswords, board games, playing cards, exercise, gardening, drawing and painting, puppet shows, having friends over for dinner, playing a musical instrument, cooking, craft, jigsaws, puzzles, table tennis and LEGO.

Take a moment to write down activities you would like to do on your own or with family and friends. After you've come up with the list, think of ways you could incorporate the ideas into the design of your home.

Playful design

'Design generosity' is the term for creating an object or space with more than just one function. Successful interior designs try to add more. When it comes to the living room, let's explore beyond the normal boundaries. Must it have a traditional sofa, or can it have multipurpose seating made from modules, inviting users to continually reconfigure it? Or why not design the living room floor to be a putting green? When you find the courage to break down the archetypes, the possibilities become limitless.

During my research I met London designer Christopher Duffy, who created the Swing Table – a dining table with swings attached, to bring the playground inside. Swinging in the chairs was an instant icebreaker. Within seconds, I felt my barriers fall down and we had a playful, fun conversation.

In the future, the home will be even smarter than us. Technology will help make life easier, better, healthier and, ultimately, happier. For instance, it will be programmed to encourage play. It might ask you or the entire family to play a game with holograms or Kinect technology projected onto any surface, or it could ask you to draw a new virtual artwork for the wall in your living room to be displayed on a giant screen. Our homes will become more flexible as the requirement for wires and cables becomes obsolete. The need for dedicated rooms with a specific purpose is disappearing, which means rooms will be more adaptable. You will be able to work or play in any room that you choose.

Some play ideas

Turn your dining table into a ping-pong table • Apply chalkboard or magnetic paint to a fridge, wall or door to play hangman or noughts and crosses (tic tac toe) • Have a camping trip in your living room, where you roast marshmallows in the fireplace, tell campfire stories and sleep in sleeping bags or makeshift tents • Bring outside objects inside, such as a swing, hammock or even a slide

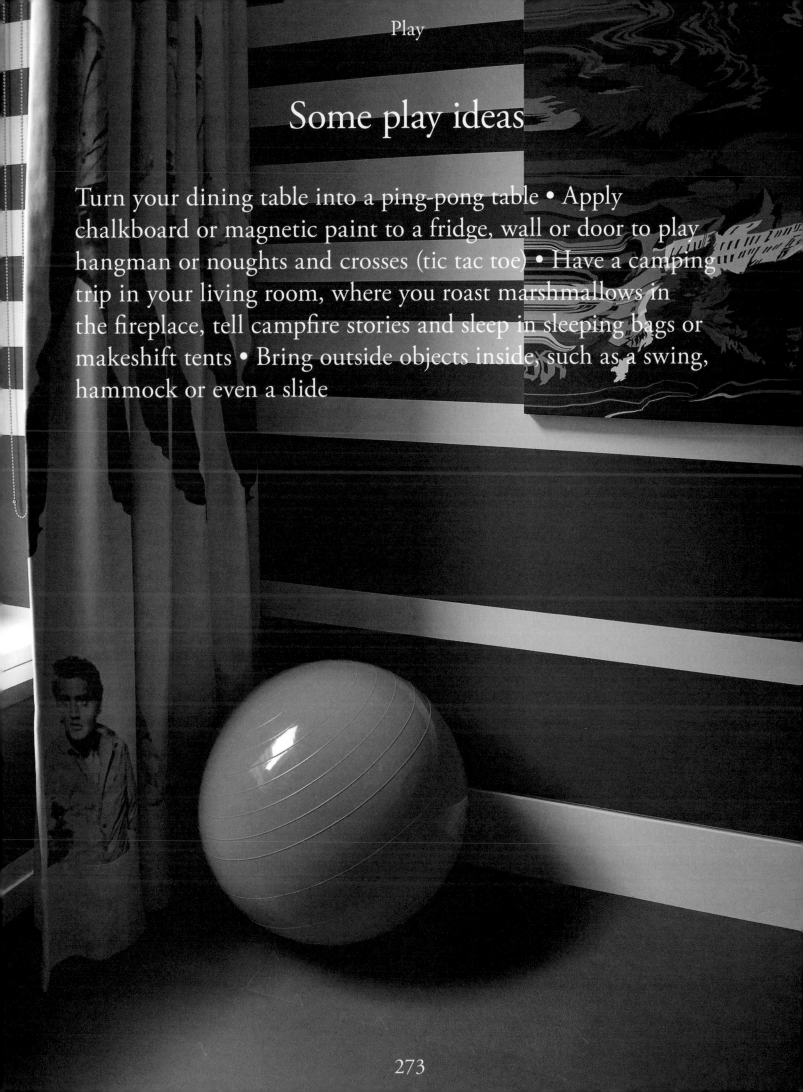

Just imagine ...

To imagine is to dream! This wonderful ability of the mind to create simulated realities and explore without abandoning the real world is one of life's great gifts. To imagine is good for you. Your home is the perfect place to free your imagination and display it in your decoration. Perhaps you often imagine yourself as an explorer or botanist who loves to travel the world by sea and you have fallen in love with a Tahitian king or princess who has come back to your homeland and you have set up home together. Or perhaps you have romantic notions of being a farmer where you grow your own crops and raise your own livestock. When you snap out of those dreams, the reality is that you probably have children around your ankles, you are working like a hamster in a wheel to pay off a mortgage and you're not going anywhere.

Some of the most successful interiors have been created through dreams. Travellers might fill their home with pictures of tall ships or beautiful found objects from the beach or forest, and use an island colour palette to inject a tropical vibe. To take the idea even further, secure rope netting to look like something that belongs on a sailing ship to replace a landing. You could hang or climb on it, or use it as a hammock to relax in. The person who dreams about living on the land might introduce an edible garden inside or out, perhaps get some chickens and fill the home with robust wooden furniture with a big beautiful farm-style kitchen. Home is where you dream and where you should play out those dreams to fit your lifestyle.

Anything is possible

Often when a task looks too complicated, we fear that we will look stupid if we get it wrong or break something. However, just look at children – they have an amazing knack for learning technology faster than adults, because they are not afraid to play around to see how things work. Kids don't fear doing something wrong. If they do, they learn from it and do it differently the next time.

I'm sure there are a lot of parents looking at some of the examples in this book and cringing at the idea of a swing or climbing wall in their home. The fear of broken bones or holes in walls might be the initial reaction, but denying the ideas presented to you will only encourage you to live with boring, unchallenging, sterile spaces. We need to move our bodies not only when outdoors, but also when we're inside. Creating a space with playful challenges and youthful imagination gives a sense that inside your household anything is possible.

Fitting play into your life can even help you solve problems, big and small. When we play, we create new neural networks in the brain. These help deal with cognitive problems. While we are playing, somehow our dilemmas are being solved in our unconscious mind. Playing for a few hours can make you feel fresh and new again and, while you're in the middle of playing, you might suddenly have a light-bulb moment and think of a solution to an issue that's been bugging you for days.

Five types of play you can include in your design:

Social play
Imaginative play
Storytelling play
Active play
Creative play

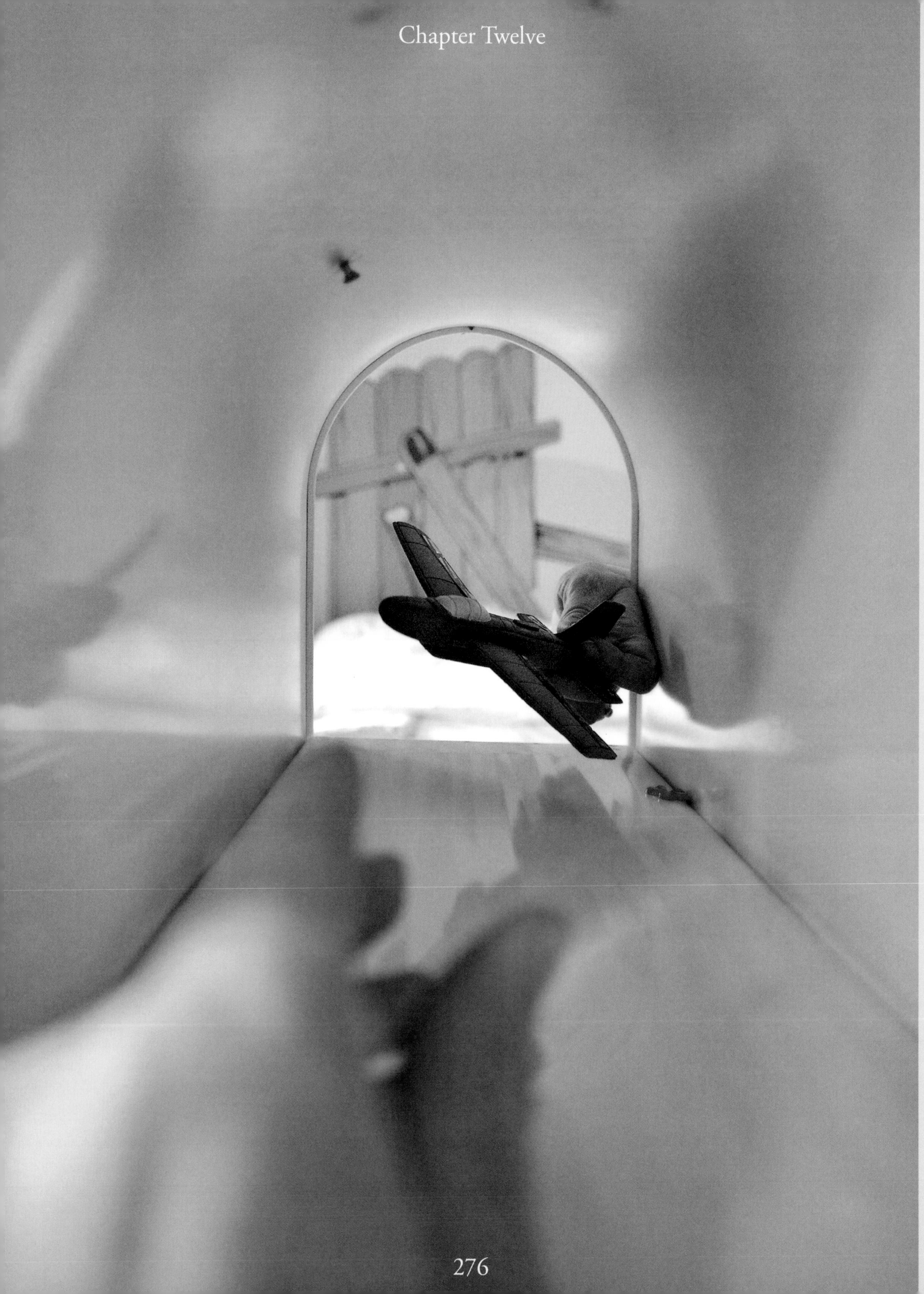

Art and creativity

It's so easy to spend an entire day consuming way too much information in our always-connected world of television, social media and on-demand everything. It has taken over our lives. That's the great thing about art; it offers an outlet from the plugged-in world. When you unplug and create something, it gives you a chance to breathe, enjoy yourself and contribute rather than consume.

Researchers are now beginning to prove what many of us have thought for some time – creativity makes us happy and promotes wellbeing. Producing art is good for you, whether it be writing, painting, singing, dancing, cooking and everything in between. Being creative can mean anything from sketching on a blank piece of paper, taking some photographs, learning how to order a glass of wine in French, getting your old guitar out of the cupboard, cooking a gourmet meal, setting up your own herb garden, knitting a scarf or just dancing and listening to music.

We need to use our hands more to create and fashion things. To get the kids and yourself away from the television or computer screen, create spaces where you can get creative, even messily creative. IKEA's Play report found that 71 per cent of parents wanted to encourage creativity at home. If you want to do this, then design spaces so your children can run riot with their imagination and flourish.

We often forget the one place children love to play is on the floor where they can spread out. This is the perfect place for cuddles, stories, games and fun. Including cushions and tactile rugs in a corner can create a comfortable spot to while away the hours together.

Make some music

Whatever age we are, from babies to senior citizens, music is a consistent part of our lives. With little effort, happy tunes make us happy. Listening to music can give us an overall feeling of wellbeing, boost our immunity and even suppress genes associated with heart disease and other conditions. Hearing your favourite tune, whatever it is, and dancing in time, makes you happy (unsurprisingly, my anthem while writing this book has been Pharrell Williams's song 'Happy'). Just before and during our favourite part of a song, our brain releases the happy chemical, dopamine. Studies by Mark Tramo, a Harvard auditory researcher, found that when people played or listened to music it increased the efficiency of oxygen consumption by the heart.

When designing your space, look at installing an integrated stereo system. There are so many great options these days that mean you don't have to have oversized boom box speakers taking up valuable floor space.

Or you could even make some music yourself. Believe it or not, playing an instrument that you have to blow into burns a significant amount of kilojoules. Just an hour a day practising will improve your health and give your lungs a great workout.

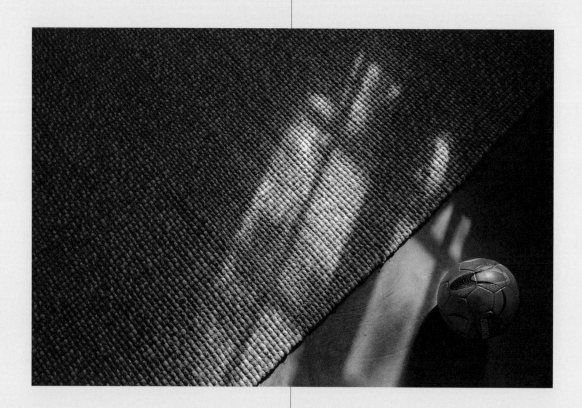

The benefits of video games

Not only are games fun, they help to stimulate our brains. The more we use our brain muscle the more active and healthier it is. Amazingly, researchers have found that simply playing board games twice a week can increase the brain speed score of primary school students by 27–32 per cent. No longer do we need to have old-fashioned board games in our home where the pieces always get lost. These games can now be played through technology, from computers to tablets and phones. Eventually our dining tables will be touchscreens, where you will be able to activate games.

I hate that my husband will read this, but it seems video games may in fact be beneficial. While they are often blamed as a cause of mental illness, isolation and obesity, studies have shown that they can also be a cure. When we play video games, endorphins are released into the brain, making us feel happier and even assisting with pain relief. Video games can also be used as a painkiller when using motion sensor technology, by helping the brain to stay busy using other senses instead of focusing on pain. It's been shown that video games played on Xbox 360, PlayStation 3 and Nintendo Wii have helped in a speedier recovery for stroke victims.

Some video games can increase intelligence by using a player's brain flexibility. A study from the University of Padua in Italy proved that playing fast-paced video games could improve the reading skills of children with dyslexia.

Four-legged friends

You can't do much better than own a pet to achieve happiness. People who own pets have been shown to have lower blood pressure and lower anxiety levels than people without pets. Pets help to ease loneliness, promote social interaction and encourage exercise and play. In fact, pets are generally great for society's happiness and wellbeing.

However, it wasn't that long ago that pets were considered a nuisance. Many buildings, rental homes and apartments still have a ban on pets. But with young people in their twenties and thirties now being less likely to have a family and more likely to own a pet, developers and building management need to accommodate this new emerging family. I believe 'no pet' policies should be banned from apartment blocks, cafés, parks and pubs. The only problem faced is that the infrastructure isn't in place to accommodate our fluffy friends. However, some friendly pubs, restaurants and cafés welcome cats and dogs.

With more people treating their pets like family members, and with less outdoor space on offer, we need to come up with some clever interior solutions. Areas to be addressed are: where they will sleep, ideas to stimulate them when the owner is not home, litter trays, food storage, somewhere to wash them, access to outside and so on. Architects and designers should be consulting not just the owner, but speaking to vets, dog trainers and groomers about what certain breeds need in order to have a happy life. A happy pet means a happy owner.

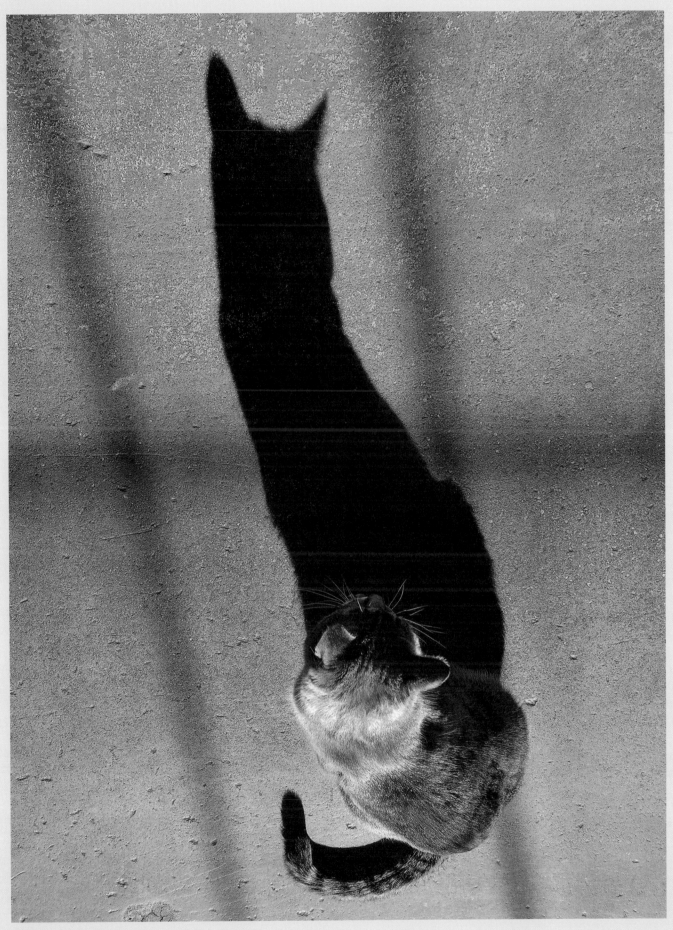

'Pets are an oasis of happiness. Hiro, my pet, is a source of constant smiles.' — Oliver Heath, chef

VOICES

GHISLAINE VIÑAS, INTERIOR DESIGNER
New York, USA

'The SkyHouse feels happy because the owners are happy people. The whole attitude is not about being fancy or serious but rather creating a home that just feels lovely. I believe in the "aesthetics of happiness" and of course this is different for different people, but this is how my clients and I interpreted it.

'I lived in the apartment with my family for three weeks because, during Hurricane Sandy, we had to evacuate our home. I really got to experience the house in a personal way and I constantly used the slide that we had installed. My two girls would wake up every morning and the clients' cats would come to their room. The girls would slide down with a cat under their arm – so pets use the slide too!

'We also installed a swing and a climbing wall in the SkyHouse, but obviously you need a lot of height and space in your home for this. The slide, swing and wall were never intended just for kids. The swing gets used all the time and so does the climbing wall.

'Crowded spaces that contain lots of knick-knacks and ornaments take up space and leave little room for movement. Uncluttering is really important for homes with kids.'

BUILDING HIGHLIGHT

There is a sculptural slide running through the entire apartment, which you use to go downstairs. There is also an indoor swing and a climbing wall.

BELIEF

Play is as much an attitude as an actual physical activity. Good design can enliven a space, bring happiness and quirkiness and make people smile.

LESSON

If you put attractive, playful elements in a home or space, people will use them – both kids and adults alike.

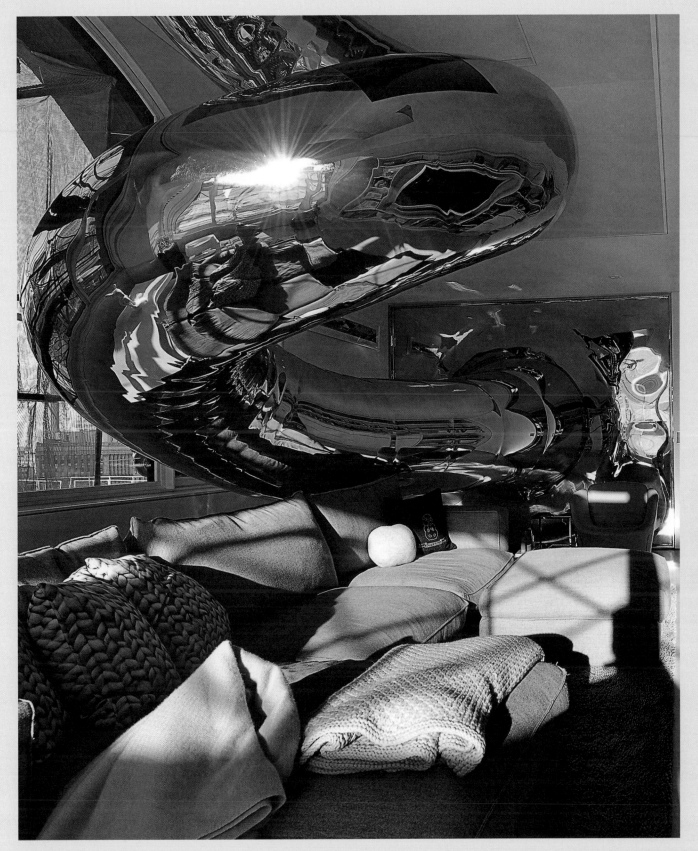

'The owners who live in the SkyHouse don't have kids but this slide was never meant for kids per se. It's a quick way to get downstairs. Everyone uses it.'
— Ghislaine Viñas

XIII

Senses

LET US RETURN THANKS TO NATURE FOR HER BOUNTY BY USING EVERY ONE OF THE SENSES SHE HAS GIVEN US …

Virginia Woolf, *The Common Reader*, 1925

See, hear, smell, touch, taste

Amanda on
people-centric design,
stimulating the senses
& the 'five a day' approach

I have always been more concerned with how the human lives in or interacts with a space or object, rather than how something looks. When designing, think first about the person and the physical connection between them and the world. The human should be the starting point. People-centric design is at the core of the way we make a happier home, building and even a city. When we put the human in the centre of design we

Senses

Fresh produce and homemade treats displayed on a table are the ultimate design element to activate all five senses.

create an emotional and intelligent space that reacts to how we live and feel. I'm always so surprised about how the human is often forgotten. Happiness is an emotion we can trigger and good design should be able to trigger our moods and affect the way we behave.

Good-quality linen sheets can change your life. Not only are they amazing to touch, they are both warm in winter and cool in summer.

The signature of a happy home is feeling emotionally and deeply rooted to the place, and there is no greater way to amplify our emotions and experiences than by stimulating our five senses: sight, touch, smell, sound and taste. They are powerful, as they can trigger our emotions to relax, heal or persuade us, and to bring us happiness. Our sensual recognition is a strong tool, because it taps into humankind's early use of the senses for survival.

Texture on a floor is your foot's best friend. Cool or warm, smooth or rough, it is up to you what mood you are trying to achieve in your space.

Awakening a person's sensual organs isn't just a romantic idea as, on a physiological level, the senses access the decision-making part of our brain, which tells us if we're in the right place at the right time and if it's a good, safe place to be – we've all had the feeling when a place makes us feel uneasy and uncomfortable.

There is a growing interest in sensory design. A unified approach, using smell, touch, taste and hearing as well as sight, will make a more creative, joyful and experiential space. Sensory design has earned its place in high-end spas and resorts. But hospitals, airports, retail environments, corporate offices and homes alike are embracing these theories to create more inviting environments.

The 'five a day' approach to life improves your mind, body and soul. The tactile, robust and natural connect us to the outdoors and give us an undeniable sense of security. Smell and taste have the power to transport us instantly back to a moment in time, whether it be an exotic holiday or eating lime marmalade with your grandparents. From playing music on your stereo to listening to running water from a fountain, sound can change your mood and uplift your spirits.

Store some of your glassware in the fridge. A chilled glass is wonderful to touch on a hot summer's day.

To create an exciting, happy space, focus on creating atmosphere by activating the senses. When it comes to giving yourself a design brief to help you tell a story, why not use this quote by 'Dr Love' – American author Leo Buscaglia – to help you: 'Too often we underestimate the power of a touch, a smile, an honest compliment, or the smallest act of caring, all of which have the potential to turn a life around.' Think about how you feel at different times of the day, and then consider how you can invoke the senses to make your life experience more rewarding.

When you're designing, never forget who you are designing for. It's your mission to activate the emotions of those who are living in the space.

SENSES
Agenda

Designer Alina Preciado has an incredible knack for knowing how to mix hard and smooth, cool and warm objects together to activate the senses.

Function versus form

A beautiful appearance is a very natural need and consequence of design, but don't start there. Always start with the humans and the story of the place, and how to make those people feel good or comfortable in that place. Architecture should be not only a visual journey but a physical experience too. Rather than focusing on aesthetics, it's far more important to work out how you are trying to affect people. Happy design is understanding that aesthetics are a consequence of all the other things we're trying to do.

We all need our home to be safe and functional before looking good. Something that starts off beautiful could quickly become an object or space you despise and think ugly if it doesn't fulfil the basics.

I'm not saying we should put less energy into what something looks like; just shift your starting point. Beauty is as important as air and water. Plato regarded vision as humanity's greatest gift. Scientists say more than half the brain is devoted to processing visual images, and 80 per cent of learning is based on visual input.

The eye of the beholder

Beauty is in the perception and interpretation of the beholder. Why is it that one person can look at someone with a wrinkled face and see it as full of character, a record of that person's life and therefore beautiful, while another person would just see the face as wizened, aged and ugly?

As pioneer American industrial designer Raymond Loewy said, 'ugliness sells badly'. Consciously or not, we are always in pursuit of beauty, whether it is for ourselves or our homes. The iPhone and iPad, designed by Sir Jonathan Ive, are classic examples of how we are willing to pay a premium for a beautifully designed machine which, technologically, is not really that different from its rivals.

I will never forget visiting designer Sir Terence Conran at his home. While we were standing around his kitchen bench, his eye caught a garlic bulb that clearly had been there for some time. It was sprouting fresh young green sprouts from the ageing purple and white bulb. He picked up the bulb and stated with such conviction how beautiful it was. I noticed that he didn't have anywhere near the same reaction to any of the other, rather more expensive, items filling his home.

What is beautiful is both subjective and objective. However, when it comes to nature – flowers, birds, butterflies, mountains, gems, trees and so on – there tends to be less disparity between what we all consider beautiful or not. On the other hand, there is much difference of opinion regarding human-made beauty.

The art of bathing is about pampering yourself. Enjoy the feeling of scrubbing your body and pouring warm water over your head.

Touch and temperature

Touch is the sense we use to connect to the material of a building and object.
Our fingertips talk to our heads and our hearts through texture, density,
temperature and weight.

The sense of touch can tell us if we are safe – it senses whether objects are sharp or smooth, hot or cold. We are drawn to the richness of natural materials in our home environment. Stone exudes an aura of strength and coolness, timber is robust and comforting, linen is light and fresh, wool is warm and cosy, leather is soft and durable, cork is gentle and tactile, metal is cool and smooth.

The temperature of a room can also totally alter the way you feel. Experiencing extremes of temperature, whether cold or hot, can make you uncomfortable and your body has to work harder to adjust. To increase productivity or comfort could be as simple as switching the temperature on the thermostat. A study from Cornell University in New York examined how different office temperatures at a large Florida insurance company would affect staff. The findings were interesting. For example, if a room was cool, with low temperatures, employees made 44 per cent more mistakes than if it was at optimal room temperature.

We are seeing examples in buildings where people are taking the hydronic heating from the floor up into feature walls. This means the floors and walls can be heated. Not only does it provide physical warmth but it also adds a psychological warmth to the space. However, when it comes to heating a space, there isn't a better device than a fireplace. If you are thinking of removing one from your home, perhaps reconsider. A fireplace is a powerful tool to activate all the senses – the warmth it provides, the sounds of it crackling, the smoky smell and the primal beauty of it. Not only does it activate the senses, it brings people together, to huddle around it, to talk, read and relax together. The fireplace is as ceremonial as it is inviting. I think it could be one of the happiest devices you could possibly have in a home.

A world of sound

After sight and touch, sound is one of the most considered elements in design.
However, most design concerned with sound is about blocking it out –
not how to enhance it!

Of course, blocking out unwanted noise is often important for our wellbeing and happiness, but we should maximise the richness of the world of sound around us as a potential source of daily inspiration.

If your home is near the sea or surrounded by wildlife, you need to capture the outside sounds and make sure they reach your home. Why would you have a soundproof bedroom if you can hear waves hitting the shoreline? Why would you block out the noise of birds singing if they are sitting in a tree outside? Let in nature's free symphony!

I lived in a very busy and noisy part of Sydney, Australia. The noise pollution below my apartment was 24/7. We had to have extra insulation and double glazing to block the noise of constant traffic and nightclubs. People who lived

on the lower floors never lasted long in the building because they were so sleep-deprived. However, there were days when I didn't want to sit in silence, and opening the windows and listening to the honking car horns and noise from below made me feel good. The sound gave me a sense of place and reminded me of the vibrant, colourful area where I lived, and why I'd chosen it.

Filling your space with sounds that make you feel good can activate happiness. It's not that we need more noise, it's that we need more sounds directed in certain areas of our buildings. As a designer, you have to set the mood. Using music in a space is a fantastic example of how positive sounds can lift an atmosphere. Remember, the sounds one does hear are just as important as the sounds one doesn't hear.

Sounds that make me happy

My husband's laughter • Waves hitting the shoreline • Rain on the roof • Thunder and lightning • A crackling fireplace • My dog barking • Coffee brewing in my coffee maker • The pop of a Champagne cork • The squeaking sound of sand underfoot • Birds chirping • Children laughing

I was in sensual heaven when I saw and touched Dietlind Wolf's ceramics. The beautiful handmade objects were the perfect backdrop for our lunch.

The power of smell

The books *Life Is Everywhere* by Sissel Tolaas and *Perfume* by Patrick Süskind changed my life. I'm serious. I suffer from 'smell blindness', meaning I can't smell things. It was only when I read *Perfume* that I realised humans had their own scent, much like a fingerprint. In *Life is Everywhere* Tolaas describes and communicates smell, which is something I have always needed my friends and family to do for me. Tolaas's book had my mind boggling. I wondered, if I could smell, would I have chosen the friends I have? Would the choices I have made in life be different? Would I have lived in the houses I have lived in?

Next to sight, smell is the most important sense we have. Remarkably, a human is able to recognise approximately 10,000 different odours and, more impressively, recall smells with 65 per cent accuracy after a year, in contrast to only 50 per cent of visuals after three months.

We know smell is important to design and that it can evoke memories, relax us and help us heal. But I want to dig deeper and consider whether, if you somehow took away all the scents from a space, it could actually help you to relax, like meditation. Should we fill our home with smells from our ancestors to help connect us to our family? Can we create scents to bring people together? Can smell change people's perception of a space? How can we include fragrances in our lives, homes and cities to make them more livable and enjoyable, and help us to trust and connect with each other?

Maybe interior designers should be hiring people like scientist, artist and nose-provocateur Sissel Tolaas to smell their clients and recommend how they should treat a building to suit the client like a perfectly fitted glove.

The familiar smell of home

Put frankly, a home that does not smell of a home is not a home at all. Coco Chanel was famously known to lavish her No. 5 perfume on the coals in her fireplace. There is something fundamental about us wanting to give our homes an appealing smell.

However, when I talk about smell for the home, I'm not talking about one of those supermarket plug-ins for the bathroom wall. A home's unique scent is made up of many things, from the fragrances you consciously add – like flowers, scented candles or essential oils and soaps – to the everyday smells, such as the food you cook and the cleaning products you use. You have chosen all of these particular smells and they reflect your own personality.

One of the most powerful tools in your 'pursuit of a happier home' arsenal is scent. Not to utilise it to the fullest is a waste. Considering aromatherapy and other olfactory-related sciences as part of your home scent can provide an enjoyable experience and, ultimately, promote the comfort and happiness of everyone within the home.

Typically, when we create spaces we only use two of our five senses, namely sight and touch. Most of us will ask what colour we should paint the entrance area, but few will ask, 'What smell will I have for the entrance?'. We are ignoring one of our most powerful senses, which has the ability to provoke our rawest emotions. In fact, 75 per cent of the emotions we generate on a daily basis are affected by smell.

Aroma and nostalgia

Smell can trigger happy memories of other smells you once experienced. When we smell a scent conjuring up treasured memories, it can make us feel content. It does appear that nostalgic smells from our childhood make us happy.

Consider all those smells that bring you comfort and happiness – maybe mangoes remind you of childhood breakfasts, roses remind you of your grandparents' garden, or perhaps the clean smell of mint reminds you of the refreshing stick of gum your father used to chew. Comfortable, domestic smells of cooking or our mother's perfume can whisk us back to a forgotten childhood world in seconds.

Scientists agree that smell and memory have a special relationship. People can often recall aromas from childhood or a distinctive odour they've only smelled once. Favourite childhood smells vary from the time you were born but usually nostalgic childhood memories relate to a smell with a positive emotion. A survey by household cleaning product company Vileda in Britain found that the Brits' favourite smells were freshly washed sheets, cut grass and home baking.

Whatever your particular nose prefers, whether it's a freshly cleaned house, aftershave, leather or the scent of cinnamon buns cooking, smells do enhance comfort and happiness. This is why retail stores work harder than homes to keep the right balance of scent wafting through their space. The more comfortable and happy the customer, the more likely they are to spend their money.

Smells that can make people happy

Fresh bread baking is said to bring out generosity • Floral scents trigger a better mood and promote social interaction with others • Licorice and cucumber not only make people happier, but make them more physically aroused as well • Peppermint cranks up motivation, energy and confidence • Citrus smells are reputed to lift your mood, with the scent of lemon oil being particularly effective – it can perk you up, reduce anxiety and give a positive impression associated with cleanliness • Lavender improves mood and relaxes you

Stimulating taste

No, I'm not going to suggest you lick your walls (although edible
wallpaper is available) or eat your bowls (they exist, too). When I talk about
taste, I'm talking about food.

Food is evocative and, because of this, it can connect people
with spaces. It can absolutely transform your experience of
a place. I mean, do you have a favourite 'divey' restaurant
that you love to go to because the food is so good? If the
food is really delicious, suddenly the run-down plastic chairs
and laminated tables seem filled with charm and character.
However, on the other side of the coin, I'm sure you have been
to an elegant, high-end restaurant that serves horrible food –
which costs more than flying to Phuket – in an environment
that's cold and unwelcoming.

Food and taste can make a space feel more inviting and
welcoming. In the kitchen, and other public areas of the home,
have fresh natural food offerings on display, such as jugs of
fresh water with slices of lemon, coffee, spicy nuts, sweet
healthy treats and fresh fruit.

When you are decorating a kitchen, don't get too
focused on hiding all the food away behind cupboard doors
and in the refrigerator. Open shelves, glass cabinets and
containers are perfect for displaying food. Don't hide it,
celebrate it! When you think about the food your family loves

and the vibe you want to create in a space, you can customise
your kitchen to fit your lifestyle. If, after school, the kids love
fresh dips to snack on, why not include a dipping bar where
you can serve salsa, hummus and so on. Or, to induce a joyful
tasting experience that promotes happy memories, how about
purchasing an ice-cream machine?

The way we experience food is a multisensory process
involving taste, aroma, the appearance of the food and the
feel of it in our mouths. How much we enjoy our food can be
influenced by the cutlery and crockery we use, from the
colour to the size, shape and weight. Cheese is said to taste
saltier if it's eaten from a knife rather than a fork, and yoghurt
apparently tastes better if it's eaten from a white spoon! Many
people like to eat dessert with a small spoon, which might be
because it's said to make food taste sweeter. Certain colours,
such as natural tones of orange, yellow, green and brown, are
said to promote appetite, while other colours, such as blue, can
inhibit it. And smaller plates and bowls also make us eat less.
However, personal taste definitely has a bearing as to what
will work for you.

'The kitchen of the future is less a spaceship but more a place for the production of food. Trends like urban farming are surpassing industrial agriculture efficiency standards fifteenfold.' — Werner Aisslinger, designer

Future sensory design

In the digital age in which we live, we need to ensure sensory design is not lost, and that we make technology work for us. It's possible to boost happier moods with light, sound and touch, and here technology can help.

A happy home needs to integrate technology and digital media by stimulating the senses and enhancing the perception of a place. Technology isn't all bad. It can actually heighten our senses. One example of this is thermochromatic materials, such as fabric, tiles or paint, that change colour according to temperature. Scientists, inventors and architects are working together to create intuitive homes that could eventually monitor the homeowner when they walk through the front door at the end of the day. The homeowner's body would be scanned to assess its state and then the computer would adjust the environment of the home to suit their needs. For example, the computer would examine body temperature and body language and it might sense that you are cold or that you have just come back from the gym. The 'smart house' would then adjust temperature, lights, music and so on to soothe you or, better yet, even carry out food preparation.

New technologies could help us change the way our homes and buildings look and feel. For example, LED wall coatings are already available that can change in colour or design, so you could be looking at a tropical beach one minute, and an alpine landscape the next.

The possibilities for creating favourite smells in the home can be way more superior than simply buying some candles, oils or flowers. It is possible now to inject your fabrics, walls, beds and pretty much anything you like with fragrance. This is called 'smart fabric' and it can be controlled and changed according to your mood. IBM believes that by 2018 computers will also be able to smell, detect infections on our breath and tell if the food we are about to eat has bacteria in it.

The ability to control and manipulate sound within a building has also become more sophisticated. There is a higher demand for designing tranquil spaces that are refuges from electronics. This is being achieved by separate television media rooms and designated spaces for mobile phone use. Natural sounds, such as water features or white noise machines, are used to muffle conversation and traffic noise.

The touchscreen is becoming more common, but a cold screen is not a touchy-feely experience. The technology we use today – computers, laptops and tablets – will be extinct by 2022. Instead, everything around your home, from doorknob and coffeepot to bench-top and wall, will have computing capabilities. If Kinect technology takes over, it would mean we will not even have to touch objects – we will simply move our hands or arms in the air to turn off our alarm clock in the morning, open doors, turn on lights, run a tap and so on. This means with technology driving us away from touching things, tactility will be all the more important to include in our designs, so we remain connected to 'reality' and the human.

VOICES

ALINA PRECIADO, DESIGNER AND ARTIST
Brooklyn, New York, USA

'I love having my bare feet against the cool concrete floors and equally love the soft hides on the floor that add warmth. Handwoven cotton towels and linen sheets feel good on my skin. Smooth leather, that collects the touches of time, is nostalgic and becomes a visual record. Feeling wood grain and cold rolled steel is a delight for contrasting texture and temperatures.

'I love a calming palette with just some pops of colour. My mind can easily become over-stimulated throughout the day, so my home has to allow my mind to rest, with shades that blend into one another harmoniously. Chimes, music, the crackling of a burning wood fire, a whistling teapot – in my home, these are the sounds of life being lived. There is a miniature chime near where my kitten plays and, when I hear it, I know she is playing; I find it a comforting sound.

'Scent for me can be seasonal, and used to alter mood and even create an aura of comfort or be cleansing. Aroma is in so many ways symphonic, when used throughout the day. Eating is one of the supreme sensual experiences in my life, and it's no wonder that I surround myself with objects of cooking, which allow me to appreciate, relive, create and remember.'

BUILDING HIGHLIGHT

A 186 square metre (2000 square foot) open and airy loft, in a nineteenth-century industrial building with killer views over Brooklyn. Smooth and rough, old and new, cool and warm, perfect and imperfect, are the winning cues here.

BELIEF

Homes live and breathe with us, and they interact with the individuals and creatures that walk about. By touching our senses we touch our heart and mind at the same time.

LESSON

New friends, loved ones, animals, food, plants, music, art, books and artefacts are all part of what makes life visually present. These things make a space feel special and help to foster happiness.

'I have a hammock hanging in my home. I think it's important to let your spirit have what it wants – mine wants long afternoons swaying back and forth and listening to music.' — Alina Preciado

XIV

Spontaneity

THE ESSENCE OF PLEASURE IS SPONTANEITY.

Germaine Greer, *The Female Eunuch*, 1970

Live in the moment

Amanda on
acting on impulse,
thinking less and feeling more
& the need for *waku-doki*

The *Oxford English Dictionary* defines spontaneity as acting on a sudden impulse or inclination without premeditation or external stimulus. Spontaneity in design is fun, optimistic and adventurous. Spontaneity isn't anything we can contrive, arrange or manipulate. By its very nature it's unforeseen and unpredictable. We can't set out and plan to be spontaneous, but it can be 'courted' or 'nurtured'. Spontaneity is a source of innovation, creativity and change. It's about thinking less and feeling more. When you

To be spontaneous in design, you have to stop thinking and just do. It's not about being rational. I mean, how many of us have thought about putting arrows above a doorway?

feel free to be spontaneous it makes you beautiful. When we are spontaneous we stop controlling and predicting. This, in my opinion, is when design gets exciting.

Dietlind Wolf has taken old frames that she has collected and placed them randomly onto her wall in her Hamburg home.

The need for control is a funny thing. When we feel like we have it we think we have power. However, perhaps this need is not freeing us or making us powerful, but is instead holding us back. More of us have found the need to create a strong sense of order in our lives and homes. Unfortunately, with this new focus so many of us have forgotten how to be spontaneous.

Rossana Orlandi has hung a cluster of Pet Es pendant lights at different heights in her Milan courtyard.

When we are spontaneous we let go of control. This doesn't come naturally to many people. With more of us feeling helpless about what is happening in the world, economically and environmentally – from wars to the rise of new superpowers and the speed of technological advances – it's natural to want control in our lives and our home. But I think we have taken this too

far. We have forgotten the one place where we should feel safe to let go is in our homes.

Most of us have busy schedules and try to balance the conflicting demands of work, family and friends. Families are operating around rosters and schedules. As helpful as they are to keep chaos at bay, we mustn't forget to sometimes be spontaneous. In a 2013 study that homeware giant IKEA carried out on Australian families, it was found that 43 per cent of parents and even 43 per cent of teenagers hadn't done anything spontaneous in the last month, and 50 per cent and 42 per cent, respectively, said they would actually have to think about what they'd do if they suddenly found they had a couple of hours spare. Spontaneity is not about suddenly buying a big family holiday – it can be as simple as spending some time together.

In this house in Belgium, a bench seat has been covered with foam, silk and a belt to hold it together.

YOLO! You only live once! Stop being so serious and make the most of your life. Do away with boring activities that don't add value. Watching the television not only eats away productivity, it drains away motivation to do something more creative or fun. Clearing out the boring activities creates space to explore. If you give yourself spare time away from the television or computer you will be more likely to act on your spontaneous ideas.

I think we all need some *waku-doki* in our lives! *Waku-doki* is the Japanese term for the feeling of anticipation you get when you are about to do something exciting and it gives you an incredible adrenaline rush (*waku-waku suru* = tremble, *doki-doki suru* = rapid heartbeats).

Interior designer Ghislaine Viñas has randomly placed miniature trees, typically used as architectural models, over an apartment wall.

SPONTANEITY
Agenda

Be brave
Show your vulnerability
Nobody's perfect
The beauty of imperfection
Spontaneous design

Be brave

I have always believed when it comes to design we need to be bold. To be spontaneous you also need to be courageous. The opposite of spontaneity is often cowardice or fear. Planning every moment of every day is the reason why spontaneity is being frozen out. Discipline and organisation allow you to be productive, but having courage and openness will help you to be spontaneous. Spontaneity relies on how much you are able to trust yourself, and happiness is intimately linked to being more self-confident, taking risks and developing more faith in decision-making.

The root of the word courage is *cor*, the Latin word for heart, meaning to show who you are with your whole heart. The reason why it's courageous to express who you really are is that you are openly showing your imperfections. You are letting people in to see what matters to you. You are being authentic in who you are. Connection with others gives meaning and purpose to our lives. But in order to have connection, we need to authentically be seen by others. We tend to fear that when people see who we really are, they may not accept us. We will always be surrounded by people who will judge us, but those people are generally living in a controlled, self-regulatory orderly fashion, which by now I hope you can see is not the answer to happiness. We want to fit in with others and be like them. But perhaps we should shift this way of thinking and focus more on simply being ourselves.

Show your vulnerability

I never understood why people found being spontaneous in design so hard. However, researcher Brené Brown, who gave a talk at a TED conference in 2010 on 'The Power of Vulnerability', made it clear. To be spontaneous makes us vulnerable. If we step out of our comfort zone, we are putting ourself in a 'vulnerable' position. We are thinking, 'Will others think it will look stupid? Will I regret it in a couple of months?' This is why we see strong fashion fads, because we are happy to take guidance from magazines who operate like fast-fashion machines. Why? Because it's safe. We know others will like the direction we have taken because they, too, have taken the same one.

Brown believes there are three things we use to protect ourselves from vulnerability: perfectionism; numbing (deadening our true feelings with things like work, food, drugs and alcohol); and foreboding (the dread that kills happiness). This, folks, has been a game-changer for me. Actually coming to terms with this made me weep for hours. Who thought writing a design book called *Happy* could have this effect!

I mean, look at the majority of buildings being designed today. They strive to look perfect. Designers don't concentrate on putting joy into them, but rather focus on the seriousness of function and beauty. We focus on the process of living, but we don't emphasise the need to feel alive. We numb any potential emotional connection to a building by making the spaces inflexible, mapping out how we 'should' live. However, as Brené Brown says, 'You can't numb emotions. When we numb our emotions we numb joy, gratitude and happiness.'

Nobody's perfect

As a society, we worry too much about being perfect. We hanker for the perfect kitchen, the perfect car or the perfect home. I think we should just wipe this word 'perfect' away. There isn't anything in the natural world that is perfect and, I can confidently say, there isn't a perfect house. It's an unattainable goal. If you strive for perfection, there isn't any room for spontaneous behaviour. Let's stop trying to achieve perfection. Let's passionately reject any notion of it. All you need to do is be true to your inner compass.

I can assure you – the more perfect you try to make your home, the more you will lose the feeling of who you are. The more of this you lose, the more people will disconnect from you and your home. All people want to do is connect with you, and they can only do that by genuinely seeing you or understanding you. As Leonard Cohen said in his song 'Anthem', if there are cracks the light can get in. Let your space be just as you are. Don't be afraid to show all the cracks.

The beauty of imperfection

A fresh loaf of hand-baked artisanal bread is, for me, the example of how imperfection is beautiful. The Roman emperor Marcus Aurelius also had an affection for crusty bread. As he put it, 'When bread is baked some parts are split at the surface, and these … have a certain fashion contrary to the purpose of the baker's art, are beautiful … and in a peculiar way excite a desire for eating.' The haphazardness arouses the appetite. This is also true when it comes to designing the home. It's the imperfections that many of us are attracted to. If only we could remember that. Don't let your design be magazine or trend-driven. Make it 'happy' driven.

We live in a time with a growing tribe of people who are infatuated with the artisanal and rustic. It's not until you accept that you and your surroundings are enough – are great, in fact – without being 'perfect', that you will be able to find real happiness. It's not a matter of convincing, but accepting. The need to convince yourself of something means there is doubt about its validity. There's no doubt that you're 'good enough'. It's something that's universally true. It's just a matter of whether or not you accept it. No convincing should be necessary.

Chapter Fourteen

Artist Tenka Gammelgaard, who works from her Copenhagen home, feels so free in her space that she is not bothered by the splatters of paint on the floor.

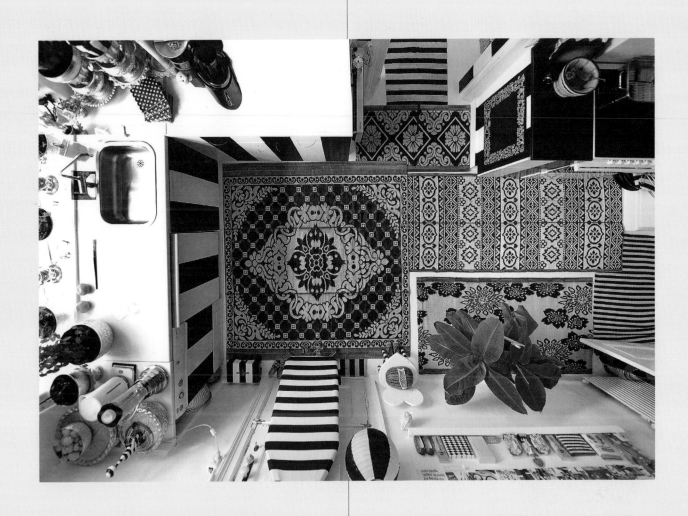

Spontaneous design

It's a tough path to act on the impulse of spontaneity because it goes against what you have set up in the perfectly designed home. But sometimes you just have to live in the moment, get a feeling and run with it.

When I scribbled with a permanent marker on my living room wall next to my newly purchased pot plant, 'My name is Rodrigou, please say hi', my husband thought I had gone down the crazy path and said, 'Why did you write that with permanent maker?' The thing is, it made me and him smile and it still does, and my response to him was to say casually, 'If we tire of it we can just paint over it'.

I loved visiting artist Tenka Gammelgaard in Copenhagen, because she seemed so free and courageous and had dared to stop striving for perfection in her beautiful home. I swear that hers was one of the warmest and most inviting homes I have ever been to. I felt the energy the minute the front door was opened. It's amazing because the apartment is painted and decorated in only black and white. Her white floorboards were covered with black splatters of paint left after painting her artwork. Most of us would be panicking and scrubbing the floors as quickly as the paint dropped. However, Tenka's floors didn't make me think, 'Oh god, look how messy she is!' Instead I couldn't get over how warm and open she was

with two complete strangers in her home. The imperfections, and the obvious spontaneous things she has done around the apartment, make the home feel alive and imbue it with a welcoming energy.

Another happy moment was when I visited the amazing SkyHouse in New York, designed by Ghislaine Viñas. In an understated blue shower was a little hole at eye height in the wall. For anyone not in the know, they would think it was just a little storage container to keep shampoo or soap in. However, when you pull the little door open there is a peekaboo tunnel and, at the end, is a perfectly framed postcard-sized vista of the Brooklyn Bridge. This wonderful, unexpected moment not only brings joy to those who discover it for the first time, but brings constant connection with the outside to the owners who live so high in the New York skyline.

Designs like this show us that it's not about how much money you have, where you live or how big your home is. It's about attitude. Embrace your situation and design your space the best you can. Why? Because it will make you happy.

323

VOICES

TENKA GAMMELGAARD, ARTIST
Copenhagen, Denmark

'I don't use my home as an art installation. It is a constantly moving story of Noa, my daughter and me. To have freedom at home is important because it means the house is never stagnant. Everything needs to keep moving. Aesthetics are important to me but it is equally important that a home has more to offer than just being beautiful and comfortable. There also should be room for fun. Humour is important within the design of the home. It's logical for me when paint falls onto my floorboards to leave it to tell a story. We never say things like, "I wish we lived here" or "If we had money we would do this". I believe this has made us enjoy our home and feel free to keep doing little things around the space.'

BUILDING HIGHLIGHT

Almost everything inside is decorated in a monochrome colour palette, from the striped kitchen units to the handles of the customised paintbrushes.

BELIEF

If you are free to have joy in your home and don't get caught up in everything inside needing to be perfect, you are free to be the very best person you can be.

LESSON

The positive and spontaneous energy you put into your home radiates out. You need to give all your energy to a space, even if it is an ugly hotel room, because you will get positive energy back.

'You must laugh eight times a day even if you live by yourself. We spontaneously write funny quotes around the house to make us smile.'
— Tenka Gammelgaard

List of sources

List of sources

— ABOUT HAPPINESS

Argyle, Michael and Hills, Peter, Oxford Happiness Questionnaire, Oxford University, 2001
http://happiness-survey.com/survey

Dockterman, Eliana, 'What makes Americans happy?', *Time*, 27 June 2013

Fokkinga, Steven, *Rich Experiences*, Delft Institute of Positive Design, Delft, 2013

Frankl, Viktor E, *Man's Search for Meaning*, 1st edition, Beacon Press, Boston, 2006

Gilbert, Daniel, *Stumbling on Happiness*, Vintage, USA, 2006

Kluger, Jeffrey, 'The happiness of pursuit', *Time*, 8–15 July 2013, pp. 22–3

Mauss, IB, Tamir, M, Anderson, CL and Savino, NS, 'Can seeking happiness make people unhappy? Paradoxical effects of valuing happiness', *Emotion*, 11 August 2011

Sheldon, Kennon M, Boehm, Julia and Lyubomirsky, Sonja, 'Variety is the spice of happiness: The hedonic adaptation prevention (HAP) model', *Oxford Handbook of Happiness*, Oxford University Press, Oxford, 2012

Van Boven, Leaf and Gilovich, Thomas, 'To do or to have? That is the question', *Journal of Personality and Social Psychology,* vol. 85, no. 6, 2003, pp. 1193–1202

— COLOUR

Carey, Tanith, 'Colour me happy: Different colours can have an effect on our moods and behaviour in rather surprising ways', *Daily Mirror*, 13 September 2012

De Lacey, Martha, 'Forget Christian Grey's Red Room of Pain, people with PURPLE bedrooms have most sex! (Unlike those poor grey-walled souls…)', *Daily Mail*, 3 September 2012

'India's Calcutta "to be painted blue"', www.bbc.co.uk, 17 February 2012
http://www.bbc.co.uk/news/world-asia-india-17071247

Kobayashi, Shigenobu, *Colour Image Scale,* Kodansha, USA, 1992

Lüscher, Max, *The Lüscher Colour Test*, Random House, New York, 1969 (first published 1949)

Madeline Gins obituary, *Telegraph*, 18 March 2014

Meerwein, Gerhard, *Colour – Communication in Architectural Space*, Birkhäuser Architecture, Basel and Boston, 1st edition, 8 June 2007

O'Connor, Zena, 'Colour psychology and colour therapy: Caveat emptor', Environment – Behaviour Studies Research Group, Faculty of Architecture, Design and Planning, University of Sydney, Australia, 11 September 2009

Pappas, Stephanie, 'Different colors describe happiness vs. depression', www.livescience.com, 8 February 2010

Schauss, Alexander G, 'The physiological effect of colour on the suppression of human aggression: Research on Baker-Miller pink', *International Journal of Biosocial Research*, 2 (7), pp. 55–64

Singh, Satyendra, 'Impact of colour on marketing', *Management Decision*, vol. 44, issue 6, pp. 783–9

— COMMUNAL LIVING

'Connections and engagement', survey by the Vancouver Foundation, June 2012, http://www.vancouverfoundation.ca/initiatives/connections-and-engagement

Cooley, Charles Horto, *On Self and Social Organisation*, University of Chicago Press, Chicago, 1998 (first published 1922)

Eisenberg, ME, Olson, RE, Neumark-Sztainer, D, Story, M, and Bearinger, LH, 'Correlations between family meals and psychosocial well-being among adolescents', *Archives of Pediatrics and Adolescent Medicine*, 158 (8), 2004, pp. 792–6

Fowler, JH and Christakis, NA, 'Cooperative behavior cascades in human social networks', *Proceedings of The National Academy of Sciences of The United States of America*, vol. 107, 2010

Gleibs, Ilka H, Morton, Thomas A, Rabinovich, Anna, Haslam, S Alexander and Helliwell, John F, 'Unpacking the hedonic paradox: a dynamic analysis of the relationships between financial capital, social capital and life satisfaction', *British Journal of Social Psychology*, 52 (1), 2013, pp. 25–43

Griffins, Jo, 'The Lonely Society?', report, Mental Health Foundation, England, 2010

Holt-Lunstad, J, Smith, TB and Layton, JB, 'Social relationships and mortality risk: A meta-analytic review', PLOS Medicine, 2010, http://www.plosmedicine.org/article/info%3Adoi%2F10.1371%2Fjournal.pmed.1000316

'The importance of family dinners VII', report from The National Center on Addiction and Substance Abuse, Columbia University, 2010

Marche, Stephen, 'Is Facebook making us lonely?', *Atlantic*, 2 April 2012

PLAYREPORT: International Summary of Research Results, IKEA, Switzerland, 2010

Stern, Y, 'Cognitive reserve and Alzheimer's disease', *Lancet Neurology*, 11 (11), 2012, pp. 1006–12

Thomas, Hannah, 'App tells you when you're happiest', *Marie Claire*, 7 November 2011

Vaillant, George E, *Triumphs of Experience*, Harvard University Press, 2012

Warrell, Margie, 'Text or talk: Is technology making you lonely?', www.forbes.com, 24 May 2012 http://www.forbes.com/sites/womensmedia/2012/05/24/text-or-talk-is-technology-making-you-lonely/

— DOWNTIME

Baird, Benjamin, Smallwood, Jonathan, Mrazek, Michael D, Kam, Julia W Y, Franklin, Michael S and Schooler, Jonathan W, 'Inspired by distraction – mind wandering facilitates creative incubation', *Psychological Science*, March 2012

'Bedroom makeover', press release, The Better Sleep Council, 2012, http://bettersleep.org/better-sleep/how-to-sleep-better/the-ideal-bedroom/bedroom-makeover

Booker, Karene, 'Good night's sleep linked to happiness', *Cornell Chronicle*, 26 April 2013, Cornell University

Cooper, Belle Beth, '10 simple, science-backed ways to be happier today', www.fastcompany.com, 6 August 2013 http://www.fastcompany.com/3015486/how-to-be-a-success-at-everything/10-simple-science-backed-ways-to-be-happier-today

Helliewell, John, Layard, Richard and Sachs, Jeffrey (eds), *World Happiness Report*, 9 September 2013, Sustainable Development Solutions Network. A Global Initiative for the United Nations, http://unsdsn.org/files/2013/09/WorldHappinessReport2013_online.pdf

Kahneman, Daniel, Kruger, Alan B, Schkade, David A, Schwarz, Norbert and Stone, Arthur A, 'A survey method for characterizing daily life experience: The Day Reconstruction Method', *Science Magazine*, vol. 306, no. 5702, 3 December 2004, pp. 1776–80.

Kaufman, Scott Barry, 'Dreams of glory', *Psychology Today*, 11 March 2014

Manocha, R, Black, D, Sarris, J and Stough, C, 'A randomized, controlled trial of meditation for work stress, anxiety and depressed mood in full-time workers', *Evidence-Based Complementary and Alternative Medicine*, vol. 2011

Niven, David, *The 100 Simple Secrets of Happy People*, Harper Collins, USA, 2009

'Reach optimum mind control', *Colors*, no. 83, 30 April 2012, http://www.colorsmagazine.com/stories/magazine/83/story/reach-optimum-mind-control

'Television and Health', California State University, Northridge, http://www.csun.edu/science/health/docs/tv&health.html.

Viet, 'The Japanese are dying to get to work [karoshi]', www.tofugu.com, 26 January 2012, http://www.tofugu.com/2012/01/26/the-japanese-are-dying-to-get-to-work-karoshi/

'What are overweight and obesity?', National Heart, Lung, and Blood Institute http://www.nhlbi.nih.gov/health/health-topics/topics/obe/printall-index.html

Zeidan, F, Johnson, SK, Gordon, NS and Goolkasian, P, 'Effects of brief and sham mindfulness meditation on mood and cardiovascular', *Journal of Alternative Complementary Medicine*, August 2010, pp. 867–73

— EDIT

Gibson, Owen, 'Shopper's eye view of ads that pass us by', *Guardian*, 19 November 2005

Leitch, Luke, 'Road map to success, Italian style', *Telegraph*, 23 October 2010

Reynolds, Siimon, *Better Than Chocolate: 50 Proven Ways to Feel Happier*, Ten Speed Press, California, 2005

— FLOW

Bar, Moshe and Neta, Maital, 'Humans prefer curved visual objects', *Psychological Science*, vol. 17, no. 8, August 2006, pp. 645–8

Bar, Moshe and Neta, Maital, 'Visual elements of subjective preference modulate activation', *Neuropsychologia*, vol. 45, issue 10, 2007, pp. 2191–2200

Booth, Robert, 'New school building designs hit by curve ban', *Guardian*, 2 October 2012

Csikszentmihalyi, Mihaly, *Finding Flow: The Psychology of Engagement with Everyday Life*, Basic Books, New York, 1998

Harte, Sunniva, *Zen Gardening*, Pavilion Books, London, 1999

Kelly, Jane-Frances and Breadon, Peter, 'Tomorrow's suburbs building flexible neighbourhoods', www.theconversation.com, 11 September 2012, http://theconversation.com/tomorrows-suburbs-building-flexible-neighbourhoods-9500

McIlroy, Anne, 'Toronto psychologist studies how the brain responds to beauty', *The Globe and Mail*, 23 February 2012

Radvansky, GA, Krawietz, SA and Tamplin, AK, 'Walking through doorways causes forgetting: Further explorations', *The Quarterly Journal of Experimental Psychology*, 2011

Ruskin, John, *The Stones of Venice. Volume the First. The Foundations*, Smith, Elder & Co, London, 1851

List of sources

Taylor, Nelson, 'Using interior design to create ample traffic flow', www.streetdirectory.com, http://www.streetdirectory.com/travel_guide/199374/interior_design/using_interior_design_to_create_ample_traffic_flow.html

— HUMOUR

Abrams, Lindsay, 'Study: forcing a smile genuinely decreases stress', *Atlantic*, 31 July 2012

Fowler, JH and Christakis, NA, 'The dynamic spread of happiness in a large social network: Longitudinal analysis over 20 years in the Framingham Heart Study', *British Medical Journal*, 5 December 2008

Gorman, James, 'Scientists hint why laughter sounds so good', *New York Times*, 13 September 2011

Lyubomirsky, Sonja, Sheldon, Kennon M and Schkade, David, 'Pursuing happiness: The architecture of sustainable change', *Review of General Psychology*, vol. 9, no. 2, 2005, pp. 111–31

'Why do we laugh?', The Naked Scientists, University of Cambridge, 26 July 2013, http://www.thenakedscientists.com/HTML/questions/question/1000179/

— LIGHTING

Boyce, Robert, *The Communications Revolution at Work: The Social, Economic and Political Impacts of Technological Change*, McGill-Queen's University Press, Montreal and Kingston, 1999

Bryson, Bill, *At Home: A Short History of Private Life*, Doubleday, UK, 2010

'Energy for buildings', CSIRO, 14 October 2011 http://www.csiro.au/Outcomes/Energy/Renewables-and-Smart-Systems/Energy-for-buildings.aspx

Innes, Emma, 'The "light shower" that could end the misery of jetlag: Airline reveals walk in chamber that resets the body's internal clock', *Daily Mail*, 5 March 2013

Karlen, Mark, Benya, James R and Spangler, Christopher, *Lighting Design Basics*, John Wiley & Sons, Canada, 2004

'Luminarium: A dynamic lighting system for contemporary environments', www.behance.com, 13 July 2012 https://www.behance.net/gallery/Luminarium/4370827

Münch, Mirjam, Linhart, Friedrich, Borisuit, Apiparn, Jaeggi, Susanne M and Scartezzini, Jean-Louis, 'Effects of prior light exposure on early evening performance, subjective sleepiness, and hormonal secretion', *Behavioral Neuroscience*, vol. 126 (1), February 2012, pp. 196–203

Nelson, Randy and Bedrosian, Tracy, 'What color is your night light? It may affect your mood', The Ohio State University Research and Innovation Communications, 6 August 2013, http://researchnews.osu.edu/archive/lightcolor.htm

Westervelt, Amy, 'How our buildings are making us sick', *Forbes*, 8 August 2012

'What is SAD?', www.sad.org.uk

— LOCATION

Benfield, Kaid, 'Why the places we live make us happy', www.citylab.com, 2 February 2012 http://www.theatlanticcities.com/arts-and-lifestyle/2012/02/why-places-we-live-make-us-happy/1122/

Bratskeir, Kate, 'The habits of supremely happy people', *Huffington Post*, 16 September 2013

Brickman P, Coates D and Janoff-Bulman R, 'Lottery winners and accident victims: Is happiness relative?', Journal of Personality and Social Psychology, 36, August 1978, pp. 917–27

Coleman, Naomi, 'Three more health benefits of being beside the sea', *Daily Mail*, http://www.dailymail.co.uk/health/article-102698/Three-health-benefits-sea.html

Cooper, Brenda, *The Futurist Magazine*, World Future Society, Maryland, September–October 2012, p. 4

Edwards, L and Torcellini, P, 'A literature review of the effects of natural light on building occupants', National Renewable Energy Laboratory, July 2002 http://www.nrel.gov/docs/fy02osti/30769.pdf

Helliewell, John, Layard, Richard and Sachs, Jeffrey (eds), *World Happiness Report*, 9 September 2013, Sustainable Development Solutions Network. A Global Initiative for the United Nations, http://unsdsn.org/files/2013/09/WorldHappinessReport2013_online.pdf

'Housing affordability: Myth or reality?', Wharton Real Estate Center Working Paper, Wharton Real Estate Center, University of Pennsylvania, 1992, http://www.census.gov/housing/census/publications/who-can-afford.pdf

Lewis, Tanya, 'Beach benefits: Oceanside living is good for health', www.livescience.com, 27 June 2013, http://www.livescience.com/37819-health-benefits-living-near-ocean.html

Leyden, Kevin M, Goldberg, Abraham and Michelbach, Philip, 'Understanding the pursuit of happiness in ten major cities', *Urban Affairs Review*, vol. 47, no. 6, November 2011, pp. 861–88

Liotta, PH and Miskel, James F, *The Real Population Bomb*, Potomac Books, Washington, 2012

Lyubomirsky, Sonja, Sheldon, Kennon M and Schkade, David, 'Pursuing happiness: The architecture of sustainable change', *Review of General Psychology*, vol. 9, no. 2, 2005, pp. 111–31

'Proposal – Bhutan's sustainability proposition: Gross National Happiness – its application and replicability', Global Economic Symposium, 2014, http://www.global-economic-symposium.org/knowledgebase/generating-winning-strategies-for-sustainable-societies/proposals/bhutan2019s-sustainability-proposition-gross-national-happiness-2013-its-application-and-replicability

— MEMORIES

Bryant, Fred B, Smart, Colette M and King, Scott P, 'Using the past to enhance the present: Boosting happiness through positive reminiscence', *Journal of Happiness Studies*, vol. 6, issue 3, 2005, pp. 227–60

How Does Your Memory Work, television broadcast, BBC Two, 2008

Howell, Ryan, 'Contrary to expectations, life experiences better use of money than material items', *San Francisco State News*, 2 April 2014, University of San Francisco

Schor, Juliet B, *The Overspent American: Why We Want What We Don't Need*, Harper Perennial, New York, 1999

— NATURE

Chang, CY and Chen, PK, 'Human response to window views and indoor plants in the workplace', *HortScience*, 40 (5), 2005, pp. 1354–9

Cooper, Brenda, *The Futurist Magazine*, World Future Society, September–October 2012, p. 4

Cooper, Brenda, 'Where the wild things are not,' World Future Society, September–October 2012, http://www.wfs.org/futurist/september-october-2012-vol-46-no-5/22nd-century-first-light/forecasts/where-wild-things-are-not

Cornish, Jeff, 'World trends & forecasts', *The Futurist Magazine*, World Future Society, March–April 2011, p. 12

Costa, Efrosini, 'Down to earth: reconnecting with the planet by walking barefoot could help you live a longer, healthier life', *Mindfoods*, Jan/Feb 2014

Eldred, Rachel, 'Climate debate: Cloudy with a change: The warming of the planet remains a hot topic on the political agenda', *Mindfoods*, Jan/Feb 2014

Eliaz, Isaac, 'The surprising health benefits of going barefoot', www.mindbodygreen.com, 27 April 2013 http://www.mindbodygreen.com/0-9099/the-surprising-health-benefits-of-going-barefoot.html

Environmental Sustainability Progress Report, City of Sydney, 2013, http://www.cityofsydney.nsw.gov.au/__data/assets/pdf_file/0004/196339/Green-Report-Quarter-2-2013-14.PDF

Fredrickson, Barbara, 'Positivity: Top-notch research reveals the 3-to-1 ratio that will change your life', *Harmony*, 29 December 2009

'The Future of Kitchens', report by IKEA, UK, 2010, http://www.ikea.com/ms/en_GB/about_ikea/press/PR_FILES/Future_kitchens_report_FINAL.pdf

Gillies, Justin and Dugger, Celia W, 'UN forecasts 10.1 billion people by century's end', *New York Times*, 3 May 2011

Kim, Gwang-Won, Jeong, Gwang-Woo et al., 'Functional neuroanatomy associated with natural and urban scenic views in the human brain: 3.0T Functional MR Imaging', *Korean Journal of Radiology*, September–October 2010, 11 (5), pp. 507–13

Kuo, Frances E and Sullivan, William C, 'Aggression and violence in the inner city: Effects of environment via mental fatigue', *Environment and Behavior*, vol. 33, no. 4, July 2001

Lehmann, Steffen, 'Green spaces can combat urban heat stress', *Adelaide Review*, February 2014

Moss, William, 'Moss in the City: Heat island effect', www.garden.org, August 2007, http://www.garden.org/urbangardening/?page=heat-island

O'Brien, Natalie, 'Threat of toxic playgrounds', *Sydney Morning Herald*, 22 January 2012

Przybylski, Andrew, Weinstein, Netta and Ryan, Richard, 'Nature makes us more caring', *Personality and Social Psychology Bulletin*, vol. 35, no. 10, October 2009, pp. 1315–29.

Ryan, Richard M, Weinstein, Netta and Bernstein, Jessey, 'Vitalizing effects of being outdoors and in nature', *Journal of Environmental Psychology*, 30 (2), 2010

Selhub, Eva M, Logan, Alan C and Wiley, ND, *Your Brain on Nature: The Science of Nature's Influence on Your Health, Happiness and Vitality*, Wiley, Australia, 2012

Than, Ke, 'Depressed? Go play in the dirt', www.livescience.com, 11 April 2007, http://www.livescience.com/7270-depressed-play-dirt.html

Todras-Whitehill, Ethan, 'Footloose and boot free: Barefoot hiking', *New York Times*, 22 September 2006

van Santen, Rutger, Khoe, Djan and Vermeer, Bram, authors of 2030, reviewed by Rick Docksai, The Futurist Magazine, World Future Society, March–April 2011, p. 55

Wagner, Cynthia G, 'Tomorrow in brief', *The Futurist Magazine*, World Future Society, May–June 2011, p. 2

List of sources

Weinstein, Netta, Bernstein, Jessey, Warren Brown, Kirk, Mastella, Louis and Gagné, Marylène, 'Spending time in nature makes people feel more alive', *Science Daily*, 2010

White, Mathew P, Alcock, Ian, Wheeler, Benedict W and Depledge, Michael H, 'Would you be happier living in a greener urban area? A fixed-effects analysis of panel data', *Psychological Science*, 23 April 2013

— ORDER

Beilock, Sian, 'Cluttered or orderly? Our surroundings shape our thinking: Physical disorder prompts creative thinking', *Psychology Today*, 14 August 2013

Duhigg, Charles, *The Power of Habit: Why We Do What We Do in Life and Business*, Random House, USA, 2012

McKay, M, Wood, JC and Brantley, J, *Dialectical Behavior Therapy Skills Workbook*, New Harbinger Publications, Inc., Oakland, 2007

Shorter Oxford English Dictionary, Oxford University Press, Oxford, 2007

— PLAY

Barron, Carrie and Barron, Alton, *The Creativity Cure: How to Build Happiness with Your Own Two Hands*, Scribner, USA, 2013

'The best predictions of 2011', *The Futurist Magazine*, World Future Society, January–February 2012

Bronson, Po, 'Is the brain like a muscle?', www.newsweek.com, 11 December 2009

Cromie, William J, 'How your brain listens to music', *Harvard University Gazette*, 13 November 1997

Guarini, Drew, '9 ways video games can be good for you', *Huffington Post*, 7 November 2013

'Physical activity improves quality of life', www.heart.org, 22 March 2013, http://www.heart.org/HEARTORG/GettingHealthy/PhysicalActivity/FitnessBasics/Physical-activity-improves-quality-of-life_UCM_307977_Article.jsp

PLAYREPORT: International Summary of Research Results, IKEA, Switzerland, 2010

Serna, Joseph, 'Study: A day of video games tops a year of therapy for dyslexic readers', *Los Angeles Times*, 1 March 2013

Southall, Ashley, 'Specialists see tools to treat pain in video games', *New York Times*, 20 April 2013

'Why play matters for adults', www.helpguide.org, April 2014, http://www.helpguide.org/life/creative_play_fun_games.htm

'World trends & forecasts', *The Futurist Magazine*, World Future Society, September–October 2011, p. 13

— SENSES

Goldworm, Samantha, 'The Power of Scent', scent.com http://1229scent.com/olfactive-branding/

Hagan, Pat, 'How the aroma of freshly baked bread makes us kinder to strangers', *Daily Mail*, 1 November 2012

Haviland-Jones, J, Rosario, HH, Wilson, P and McGuire, TR, 'An environmental approach to positive emotion: Flowers', *Evolutionary Psychology*, 2005 (3)

Lacey, Miriam, '5 scents that are guaranteed to make you happier', www.popsugar.com.au, 14 March 2012 http://www.popsugar.com.au/beauty/5-Scents-Make-You-Happy-Reduce-Anxiety-22183679

Lindstroem, Martin, *Brand Sense: Build Powerful Brands through Touch, Taste, Smell, Sight and Sound*, Free Press, USA, 2005

Mahoney, Sarah, '9 aromatherapy health cures: The best scents to help boost your memory, mood, energy, and libido', *Prevention*, December 2012

Prigg, Mark, 'How your phone could be able to smell, hear and taste by 2018: IBM reveals its vision for the future of technology', *Daily Mail*, 18 December 2012

Reynolds, Emma, 'Our favourite smells', *Daily Mail*, 11 June 2012

— SPONTANEITY

Brown, Brené, 'Daring greatly: How the courage to be vulnerable transforms the way we live, love, parent, and lead', Penguin Group, USA, 2013

Marcus Aurelius, *Meditations*, Penguin Classics, 2006 edition

Shorter Oxford English Dictionary, Oxford University Press, Oxford, 2007

The Time to Live Report: Lifting the roof on Australian family life at home, IKEA, Australia, 2013

Urban Dictionary, www.urbandictionary.com

The Happy Poll can be found at http://esurv.org/online-survey.php?surveyID=OCHEFG_36f538ca

Happy

Location credits

Endpapers (front and back), pages 22, 23, 28, 29, 126, 226, 313
Augustin und Frank Architekten
www.augustinundfrank.de

Pages 1, 19, 23, 24, 25, 40, 41, 266, 267
Matali Crasset
www.matalicrasset.com

Pages 8, 105, 179
Kawaiian Lion
www.kawaiianlion.bigcartel.com

Pages 21, 304, 305
Werner Aisslinger
www.aisslinger.de

Pages 23, 109, 180, 181, 188, 189, 228, 318
Mark Tuckey
www.marktuckey.com.au

Pages 28, 31, 36, 38, 95, 120, 201, 235, 308, 314, 321
Jean-Christophe Aumas
www.voicivoila.com

Pages 30, 159, 298, 302, 303, 315
Dietlind Wolf
www.krop.com/dietlindwolf

Pages 32, 33, 34, 35, 54, 140, 141, 142, 143, 164, 184, 246, 260, 270, 273, 276, 277, 281, 316
Ghislaine Viñas
www.gvinteriors.com

Pages 39, 78, 168, 182, 183, 193, 211, 254, 255
Piero Lissoni
www.lissoniassociati.com

Pages 42, 45, 50, 65
Hiroyuki Shinozaki Architects
www.shnzk.com

Pages 47, 56, 265, 267
Marc Sadler
www.marcsadler.it

Pages 48, 55, 83, 98, 165, 166, 167, 169
Lee Broom
www.leebroom.com

Pages 49, 111
Vipp
ww.vipp.com

Pages 51, 159, 250, 251, 252, 253
Anja Thede
www.a-thede.de

Page 57
Emily Gray & Marius Haverkamp
www.gray-label.com

Pages 58, 59, 263
Studio R U I M
www.xxruim.com

Pages 60, 61
Clare Cousins
www.clarecousins.com.au

Pages 66, 69, 71, 72, 73, 74, 75, 76, 89, 248, 285
Bergdorf
www.bergdorf.org

Pages 79, 80, 81, 139
Emma Persson Lagerberg
www.emmaperssonlagerberg.blogspot.com

Pages 82, 230, 231, 238, 311, 315
51N4E
www.51n4e.com
Art Economy
www.arteconomy.be

Pages 85, 107, 114, 119, 122, 123, 219, 237
Leeton Pointon Architects
www.leetonpointon.com
Susi Leeton Architects
www.susileeton.com.au

Pages 86, 127, 130, 131, 132, 161
Bureau de change
www.b-de-c.com
Made.com
www.made.com

Page 87
Lloyd Hotel & Cultural Embassy
www.lloydhotel.com

Pages 90, 93, 96, 97, 102, 113
Arno Brandlhuber
www.brandlhuber.com

Pages 100, 101, 104, 110, 144
NORM
www.normcph.com

Pages 106, 108
Jan Rösler Architekten
www.janroesler.de

Location credits

Pages 117, 121, 124, 216, 232, 233, 245, 247
Leeton Pointon Architects
www.leetonpointon.com

Pages 121, 128, 129, 132, 133, 225
Renzi Design
www.renzidesign.com.au

Pages 134, 146, 147, 150, 151, 177, 256, 257
McBride Charles Ryan
www.mcbridecharlesryan.com.au

Pages 137, 148, 320, 322, 323, 325
Tenka Gammelgaard
www.tenka.dk

Pages 149, 267
Cool Edies
www.cooledies.com

Pages 152, 157, 158, 172, 173
Betillon / Dorval-Bory
www.betillondorvalbory.tumblr.com

Pages 155, 294, 295
25hours hotel Zurich West
www.25hours-hotels.com

Pages 162, 202, 203, 204, 206, 208, 209, 213, 214, 215
Jo Wood Interiors
www.jowoodinteriors.com
Urban Infill
www.urbfill.com

Page 186
Andreas Krüger

Pages 190, 191, 243, endpapers (back)
Andrew Maynard Architects
www.maynardarchitects.com

Page 195
Welcome Beyond
www.welcomebeyond.com

Pages 199, 282, 288, 292, 293, 296, 299, 307
Alina Preciado
www.dargitane.com

Pages 207, 259
Stephen Bayley
www.stephenbayley.com

Pages 221, 234
Daniel Bell Garden Design
www.danielbell.se

Pages 222, 223
MLRP
www.mlrp.dk

Page 241
Owner: Marcus Luft
Builder: Fridolin Gottstein

Page 244
ON Design
www.ondesign.co.jp

Pages 272, 287
Maarten de Ceulaer
www.maartendeceulaer.com

Page 274
Duffy London
www.duffylondon.com

Page 315
Rossana Orlandi
www.rossanaorlandi.com

Page 334
Art Economy
www.arteconomy.be

Acknowledgments

Thank you to Diana Hill for being the first to believe in *Happy*, Ariana Klepac for being an editor goddess, and to all the rest of the team at Murdoch Books who have worked on this book.

To my AMAZING photographer who travelled the world with me and had to put up with me as a travel companion. Who slept on my sofa, who drove us through Italy, who was patient with me accidently jumping into so many shots, who comforted me at one of my saddest times and who put up with my organisational skills in planning our journey. I adore you.

Thank you to my very patient Oliver Heath who has carried out more house duties than me during the writing of this book. I love you. To my favourite blonde, Hiro Heath, for being understanding in having to forgo some walks. Thanks to my mum, Wendy Talbot, who is strong, beautiful and can do a mean foxtrot. To Lorraine Lock and Nikki Davies, thank you for being awesome and a huge support.

Thank you to Ole Truderung for having a wonderful vision in designing *Happy*. I feel so lucky to have worked with you on this book. You are a very special talent.

Thank you to the amazing new and old friends we met along the way who were so hospitable. Thank you Donatella Burn for hosting us in Milan and accompanying us to Tuscany; to the incredibly generous Mirko Beetschen and Stephane Houlmann; and to my old London buddies David and Sarah Ellis, who made us feel so welcome and showed us a home full of fun.

My biggest thank you must go to everyone who is in this book. I could never have done it without you. You are all so inspiring and the reason why I love my job.

THANK YOU!

Published in 2014 by Murdoch Books, an imprint of Allen & Unwin

Murdoch Books Australia
83 Alexander Street
Crows Nest NSW 2065
Phone: +61 (0)2 8425 0100
Fax: +61 (0)2 9906 2218
www.murdochbooks.com.au
info@murdochbooks.com.au

Murdoch Books UK
Erico House, 6th Floor
93–99 Upper Richmond Road
Putney, London SW15 2TG
Phone: +44 (0) 20 8785 5995
www.murdochbooks.co.uk
info@murdochbooks.co.uk

For Corporate Orders & Custom Publishing contact Noel Hammond,
National Business Development Manager, Murdoch Books Australia

Publisher: Diana Hill
Designer: Ole A. H. Truderung — Strategische Systeme
Project Editor: Ariana Klepac
Editorial Managers: Claire Grady & Virginia Birch
Production Manager: Mary Bjelobrk

A cataloguing-in-publication entry is available from the catalogue of the
National Library of Australia at www.nla.gov.au.

ISBN 978 1 74336 054 5 Australia
ISBN 978 1 74336 061 3 UK

A catalogue record for this book is available from the British Library.

Colour reproduction by Splitting Image Colour Studio Pty Ltd,
Clayton, Victoria
Printed by 1010 Printing International Limited, China